REAL PONIES
DON'T GO OINK!

REAL PONIES DON'T GO OINK!

Patrick F. McManus

An Owl Book
Henry Holt and Company · New York

Henry Holt and Company, LLC
Publishers since 1866
115 West 18th Street
New York, New York 10011

Henry Holt® is a registered
trademark of Henry Holt and Company, LLC.

Library of Congress Cataloging-in-Publication Data
McManus, Patrick F.
Real ponies don't go oink! / Patrick F. McManus.—1st ed.
p.   cm.
ISBN 0-8050-1651-1
ISBN 0-8050-2107-8 (An Owl Book: pbk)
I. Title.
PN6162.M3498   1991   90-29893
814'.54—dc20   CIP

Henry Holt books are available for special promotions and
premiums. For details contact: Director, Special Markets.

First published in hardcover in 1991 by
Henry Holt and Company

First Owl Books Edition 1992

Designed by Claire Vaccaro

Printed in the United States of America

19   20   18

Most of the previously published stories in this book originally appeared
in *Outdoor Life*, in slightly different form, with the exception of "Pouring
My Own," which was first published in *Spokane Magazine,* and "The Late
Great Fourth," which was first published in *True Magazine*.

Contents

REAL PONIES
DON'T GO OINK!

Controlling My Life

I just read a book on how to get control of my time and therefore of my life. My time has always had a tendency to slip away from me and do as it pleases. My life follows it, like a puppy after an untrained bird dog. Come night, my life shows up, usually covered with mud and full of stickers, exhausted but grinning happily. My time never returns. That is why I read this book on how to get control of my time and my life.

The book claimed that the key to controlling your time and life is to make a list of all the things you want to accomplish during the day, the week, and the year. Things you wish to accomplish are listed according to their level of importance in categories labeled A, B, and C. Under A, you place the things that have top priority for the day, under B, the things you really should take care of that day or in the immediate future, and under C, the things that you might do sometime next century.

The system sounded wonderful. Finally, I had a way to actually control those two rascals, my time and my life. Time would no longer merely slip away. I'd grab it by the neck, squeeze every second out of it, and toss the empty skin over my shoulder. My life would become a thing of discipline, methodically achieving great accomplishment after great accomplishment. I sat down to start my list.

Right off I was stumped. I needed to think of a great accomplishment to list first under A. Writing the Great American Novel would be a good one, I thought. But it would probably take too long. It took me two months to read *Moby-Dick*. How long would it take me to write it? Scratch that idea.

My wife, Bun, walked in. "Why are you sitting there staring out the window?"

"I'm trying to control my life," I said.

"Oh good," she said.

"Can you think of something great for me to accomplish?"

"How about putting up the shelf in the pantry like I asked you?"

"No good. Too trivial. It's low C at best, if it even makes the list. Speaking of lists, where's a pencil?"

"Go look in the junk drawer."

I looked in the junk drawer, but all I could find was the stub of a pencil, with the eraser worn down flat. Not only do you need a good pencil to get your life under control, you need a good eraser.

"I'm going down to the store and buy a new pencil," I told Bun.

"I hope getting your life under control isn't going to run into a lot of expense," she said.

On the way to the store, I bumped into my friend Retch Sweeney. "Where you going?" he asked.

"Down to the store to buy a pencil," I said. "I'm getting my life under control."

"What's it been doing?" he asked.

"Just the usual," I said. "As a result, I never get anything accomplished."

"I never accomplish anything either," he said. "Why don't we stop by Kelly's for a beer, and you can tell me how to get my life under control, too."

"Okay."

We went into Kelly's Bar & Grill. Kelly himself was working the bar. Tiffany, the waitress, was arm wrestling Milt Logan for double her tip or nothing. Two candles were situated so that the loser got his hand forced down onto one of them. Tiffany was winning. "Stop! Stop!" screamed Milt. "I give up!"

Kelly chuckled. "Good thing I don't let Tiffany light the candles," he said. "Otherwise, every one of you bums would have the hair burnt off the back of your hands."

"Oh, yeah?" Retch said to Kelly. "Well, me and Pat can beat the socks off you and Tiffany at pool."

"You think so, do you?" Kelly said, vaulting over the bar. "Rack 'em up, Tiff. How much per game?"

By the end of a few games of pool, getting my life under control had already cost me twelve dollars. Then Old Crabby Walters came over and asked if Retch and I wanted to see his new boat. "Sure," I said. "I love to look at boats. But we better hurry. It's starting to get dark."

We went down to the marina to look at Crabby's boat. I

would have guessed its vintage at early seventeenth century, except it was made out of aluminum. The motor looked prehistoric.

"You fix this up, Crabby, it'll be a pretty fair boat," Retch said.

"Jumpin' Jehoshaphat!" cried Crabby. "It's already fixed up!"

"Oh," Retch said. "And a mighty nice job of it, too."

"Thanks," Crabby said. "You boys hop in and I'll take you for a little spin."

"Gee, it's pretty darn cold out and it's almost dark," I said. "And the wind is coming up."

"Jumpin' Jehoshaphat!" cried Crabby. "What kind of wimps are you two? Hop in!"

Retch and I hopped in, trying to avoid the rusty gas tanks. The whole boat smelled of gas. Crabby jerked on the starter cord no more than fifty times before the motor roared to life somewhere beneath a cloud of smoke. I wasn't sure whether the motor was running or on fire, but Crabby soon emerged from the cloud, a big grin on his face. "Purrs like a kitten, don't it?"

We bolted out onto the lake, the motor coughing and spitting and occasionally screaming in agony. A couple hundred yards from shore it died. "Just have to adjust the throttle a little," Crabby said calmly, removing the motor cover and tossing it with a clatter into the bottom of the boat.

The wind had picked up. Icy waves began to toss the boat this way and that, mostly that, which was away from land. Darkness had clamped a lid on the lake.

"One of you boys got a flashlight on you?" Crabby asked. "I can't see a dad-blamed thing."

"Not me," Retch said, staring at the waves.

"Me neither," I said. "I just went out to buy a pencil." The situation was getting on my nerves.

"Well, no matter," Crabby said. "I got an old gas lantern in here somewheres. Ah, there it is. I'll get us some light in here in a sec."

"Wait!" I said. "Do you think it's such a good idea to light a lantern with all this gas in here?" Retch inched his way toward the bow of the boat. I inched after him.

"No problem," Crabby said. He touched a match to the lantern. Flames shot up six feet. Retch and I stared in horror at the rusty gas tanks, now brightly illuminated so we could study in detail the full extent of their deterioration.

"*JUMP—!*" cried Crabby.

Retch and I jumped for our lives, leaving poor Crabby to fend for himself. He never even heard the splashes or the muffled shrieks so closely associated with plunges into ice water. I surfaced right next to the boat, expecting to see Crabby doing an imitation of a Roman candle. But he was just standing there with the lantern turned down to a modest glow.

"—pin' Jehoshaphat!" he muttered, completing his favorite oath. "One of these days I'm going to buy me a new lantern. Now if one of you boys would . . . where'd you go?"

Crabby eventually got the motor going, and towed Retch and me back to the dock. Then he drove us to Kelly's to thaw out. Naturally, the boys wanted to hear about our adventure. Crabby told a long, involved story about how he had saved our lives, starting with when he was five years old. Then Retch had to arm wrestle Tiffany for double the tip or nothing, but, with Kelly gone, this time with the candles lighted. Finally, he drove me home.

"How long do you suppose before the hair grows in again?" he asked, blowing on the back of his hand.

"Probably a couple of months," I said. "Who cares? I lost five bucks betting you could take Tiffany." Getting my life under control had already cost me seventeen dollars, and I was barely started.

When I got home, Bun was already in bed. Where does the time go?

Next morning I got up bright and early and sat down to do some serious work on controlling my life.

"Where's a pencil?" I asked Bun.

Strange Meets
Matilda Jean

I had always wanted to have a dog I could be proud of, but instead I had Strange. All my friends were proud of their dogs. They bragged constantly about how Sport or Biff or Rags or Pal had run off a burglar, saved a little girl from drowning, brought in their father's newspaper, warned the family just in time that the house was on fire, rounded up cows, pointed pheasants, retrieved ducks, and performed such amazing and entertaining tricks that I had a hard time believing the dog didn't have a movie contract.

Strange, on the other hand, would have welcomed burglars with open paws, and stood watch while they looted the house. He never saved anybody from anything. He enjoyed chasing cows, but merely for the sport. He considered pointing impolite. If he retrieved a duck, it was for his own use. Any tricks he knew he kept to himself.

He was a connoisseur of the disgusting. He turned up his nose at my grandmother's cooking, then dined happily on cow chips, year-old roadkill, and the awful offal of neighborhood butcherings. Occasionally, he scrawled his territorial signature on the leg of a complete stranger, as though it were a mobile fireplug. (*"Bad dog! Sorry about your pant leg, mister. Now, as I was saying, would it be all right if I fish the crick behind your place? I'll close the gates."*) Strange was also an enthusiastic crotch-sniffer, causing visitors to gyrate like belly dancers in their efforts to escape his probing nose, all the while trying to carry on a normal conversation, as if nothing embarrassing were happening down below.

Concern for the sensibilities of the reader prevents me from mentioning some of my dog's more disgusting hobbies, except to say they involved highly noxious fumes, chickens, human legs, embarrassing itch, and various slurpy aspects of what passes for dog hygiene. Strange apparently held the view that his hobbies were vastly entertaining to the public at large. Whenever we had dinner guests he would run through his repertoire of the disgusting in front of the dining-room window.

"How did you like that one?" he would ask, smiling in at us, as though expecting a standing ovation.

"No dessert for me, thanks," our guests would respond. Strange was a major social liability.

"There's nothing worse," my grandmother once commented, "than an egg-sucking dog."

"Strange don't suck eggs," I said proudly, desperate to find something favorable about my dog.

"I stand corrected," Gram said. "There is something worse." She and Strange didn't relate well.

We never thought of Strange as *our* dog. He was his own

dog. What I disliked most about him was his arrogance. If I threw a stick and told him "Fetch," he would give me this insolent stare, which said, "Fetch it yourself, dumbo. You threw it." Then he would flip a cigarette butt at me, blow out a stream of smoke, and slouch back into his doghouse. (Well no, of course, he didn't really smoke cigarettes, but that was the essence of his attitude, as though he had watched too many movies about hard-boiled detectives.) Strange clearly thought of himself as a big tough canine, even though he was probably the smallest dog in our neighborhood. He was rather sickly looking, too, with chronically bloodshot eyes and a loose, leering mouth. Eating year-old roadkill probably does that to you. I can't imagine what a vet would have recommended for a dog like Strange. Probably a parole officer.

Strange swaggered about our place as though he owned it. You could almost see him thinking, "I won this house in a crap game, and there ain't nobody telling me what to do on my own property." After one of his particularly obnoxious offenses, often involving deadly toxic fumes, my grandmother would grab him by two handfuls of hide and send him flying outside, whereupon Strange would turn and snarl at her, "Try that again, old woman, and you'll hear from my lawyer." Then he would take out his vengeance on a chicken or squirrel or anything he could find that was smaller than himself. He reigned supreme in the confines of our yard.

Then one day my sister, Troll, brought home a huge yellow tomcat. The cat was half as big as she was. It was the cat version of an offensive all-pro tackle, and looked as if it ate scrap iron for breakfast. Its purr rattled dishes in the cupboard. Sex education not yet having been introduced in our schools, my sister named the burly yellow beast *Matilda Jean!* I was so disgusted with the name I almost gagged, but she said it was her cat, she'd name it anything she pleased.

"How do you know it's a tomcat, anyway?" she sniffed at me.

Troll had me there. We went to the same school. It just *looked* like a tom.

Although Matilda Jean was thoroughly gentle and affectionate with members of the family, he obviously was a fighter. One ear had been gnawed half off, patches of fur were missing, and numerous scars recorded the history of a violent, brawling past. Matilda Jean lounged around the house all the first day at his new home, but that evening he got up, stretched, rippled his shoulder and neck muscles like yellow waves on a pond, strode to the door, and asked to be let out.

Later that night, as we were preparing for bed, a terrible cat fight broke out on the roof of our house. It raged back and forth over the roof, up one side and down the other. We rushed out to save poor Matilda Jean and chase off the intruder. We needn't have bothered. Suddenly, a tangled, writhing, screeching knot of cats toppled off the roof and thumped to the ground. Matilda Jean landed on his back at the bottom and for a moment was stunned. The intruder, a big black-and-white model owned by our neighbors, saw its chance. It pulled itself together, a fairly complicated task, matching up the various parts, and streaked off into the night. Matilda Jean got up, rippled his muscles, and climbed back to the roof, apparently taking upon himself the responsibility of protecting us from any shifty-eyed scoundrels who might happen by.

Strange had been away from home for two days. We thought nothing of it, since he regularly went off carousing with his cronies. When he didn't show up the day after the cat fight, however, I began to worry. He wasn't much of a dog, but he was all the dog I had. "Maybe something happened to him," I said to Gram.

"There you go again," she said, "getting my hopes up."

I went out to see if Strange had slipped in unnoticed and was sacked out in his doghouse sleeping off a hangover. The doghouse was empty. Then I saw him, sauntering down the road, occasionally glancing over his shoulder to check whether he was being tailed, possibly by the vice squad. He stopped at the gate and scanned the yard in search of a chicken or squirrel available for assault and battery. The yard was empty.

Matilda Jean peered intently down from the roof, on the lookout for shifty-eyed scoundrels. Strange, of course, fit the description. The cat dropped to the ground a few feet from the startled dog.

It is difficult to know what goes through a dog's mind, but I suspect the few cognitive processes available to Strange were assessing the situation something like this: *A cat! What's a fool cat doing on my property? Dogs chase cats. I'm a dog. Therefore, I will chase this cat and teach it a good lesson. The cat will start running any second. Get ready!*

Matilda Jean didn't start running. His back arched, his hair bristled, his tail lashed back and forth like a ragged yellow whip.

Strange eyed the cat calmly. *So, it's a fight the pussycat wants. Well, he's come to the right place!* He clamped a cigar in his teeth, struck a match on the seat of his pants, lit the cigar, and flicked the match away. Eyes squinted, he smiled grimly around the cigar as he loosened the guns in his holsters. *Draw, cat!*

"Woof!" he said.

"KILLLLLLLLLLLLLL!" Matilda Jean screamed.

Finally, my dog did something I could brag about. The next day at school I casually mentioned that my dog was really something. "You won't believe what he did last night."

My friends stared at me in astonishment. "You don't mean Strange, do you?" one of them said. "You got another dog?"

"Nope!" I said. "It was Strange. What happened, Troll brought home this big old tomcat, and Strange and it got in a heck of a fight. And you won't believe this, but right in the middle of the fight, the cat and Strange went right up that tamarack tree in our yard. Strange raced up it just like a squirrel. Man, it was something to see! That ol' cat was so surprised it almost fell out of the tree!"

"Wow!" somebody said. "No kidding, you mean Strange actually chased a cat up a tree and climbed up after it?"

People always get so distracted by petty details. What did it matter, who chased whom? The important thing was, *my dog climbed a tree!*

Tough Guys Don't Bird

You've heard the expression "Tough guys don't bird." You haven't? Well, forget I mentioned it. The point is I'm a pretty tough guy, and I bird. I'm a birder, a bird watcher. I watch birds. So there. I said it and I'm glad.

All my life I've been interested in birds. A person can learn a lot from watching birds, especially if you're into sitting on power-line wires or snatching insects out of the air with your beak. Only kidding about that. The truth is I've never watched a bird do anything that I've personally found useful. I really don't know why I watch birds. It's kind of stupid, if you think about it.

Birding doesn't even make good conversation. I went down for lunch with the guys at Kelly's Bar & Grill, and casually mentioned that I spotted a red-shafted flicker in my backyard.

"Cripes!" Ed Riley said. "Not while I'm eating!"

"Boy, I hope you stomped that sucker," Bart Slade growled.
"Traipsing right through your backyard, was he? Probably
one of them dopers. Dang dopers and preverts are takin' over
the world! What did this fella look like—short, tall, what, in
case I catch him hanging around my place?"

"Short," I said. "Real short. With a pointy nose."

Actually, I'd just as soon the guys at Kelly's didn't know
I'm a birder.

Even when I was a child my interest in birds didn't re-
ceive much encouragement. "Hey, Ma, guess what!" I'd
shout, running into the house. "The baby robins are starting to fly from their nest!"

"So? You expected they'd shinny down the tree trunk?
Now go wash for supper."

The first actual encouragement my birding ever received
was from my wife, Bun. One birthday she gave me a book
titled *Field Guide to the Birds of North America*. I rushed out with
my field guide and tried to identify the first bird I saw, a
little brown-and-gray chap. "Hey, no problem," I said to
myself. "I'll just thumb through the book until I find a little
brown-and-gray bird." The book was half filled with little
brown-and-gray kinds of birds, dozens and dozens of them,
each differing from its fellows only by a speck of black, yellow, or white, a fat beak or a thin beak, a perky tail or a
droopy tail. I immediately classified all these species as Drab
Little Birds, and closed the book on them.

Excluding Drab Little Birds, I eventually got to know
most of the species in our region of the country. Oh, occasionally I make an erroneous identification. Once, hiking
with Bun along the river, I mistook an immature bald eagle
for a spruce grouse. It was embarrassing. Who even expects
a bald eagle to be immature? Anyway, I spotted this bird

high up in a tree and made a snap identification of it for Bun, just to impress her.

"Spruce grouse," I said, pointing.

At that moment the bird had the unmitigated gall to glide down over the river and snatch up a snack for lunch.

"I didn't know grouse caught fish," Bun said.

"Sometimes they do," I explained. "It's rare, though. Few people ever witness a grouse catching a fish with its talons. This is really a special experience, something I think we should share just between the two of us and never tell anyone else about."

"I think I'll tell."

I try not to get personally involved with the birds I watch. Who wants a meaningful relationship with a bird, anyway? What can it lead to? Trouble, that's what.

One summer a Drab Little Bird almost drove me crazy. While the river was down during the winter, I had buried concrete blocks in the sand with chains attached to them. I then hooked the chains to two-by-four boards so that when the water came back up the free ends of the chains would float to the surface. I planned to use the chains to anchor a classy new dock I intended to build.

The river rose in the spring, the boards floated the chains up with the rising water, and everything was ready for me to carefully craft a fine new dock. First, however, I had to take care of some complicated wiring problems in the innards of my boat. One morning I looked out the window and saw a Drab Little Bird bobbing about on one of my chain boards. He bobbed his tail up and down about twice a second, and with each bob he emitted a shrill sound, something like "Jeeet!" Although I had long before given up trying to identify Drab Little Birds, I guessed this fellow was a member of the dipper crowd, so named because of the constant dipping of the tail.

"Oh, he's so cute," Bun chirped. "Look at the way he dips up and down. It looks like he's doing deep knee bends."

I went out to undertake the nerve-fraying task of rewiring my boat, parked a short distance from the dipper's board. "Jeeet jeeet jeeet jeeet," went the little dipper. "Jeeet jeeet jeeet jeeet . . ." It is surprising how quickly continuous jeeet-jeeet-jeeeting can erode one's sanity. When I could stand it no longer, I climbed out of the boat, selected a good throwing stone, and hurled it in the general direction of the dipper. He flew off to a rocky point and waited until I climbed back into the boat and immersed myself in its innards. Then he flew back to his board: Jeeet jeeet jeeet jeeet jeeet . . .

Every morning the dipper would arrive at the board, no doubt carrying a sack lunch, and begin his endless exercising and jeeet-jeeet-jeeeting. This bird was making a career out of driving me crazy. I started having nightmares in which he starred.

"I can't stand that dip any longer," I growled at Bun one morning. "I have yelled at him, put curses on him, and thrown rocks at him, and he still insists on driving me crazy. Now I'm going to take drastic measures."

"You don't mean. . . !"

"That's exactly what I do mean. I'm going to build the dock! Then he won't have his board to stand on anymore."

I threw the dock together in two days, working with the furious energy that comes only from near-madness. The results weren't pretty. Visitors who saw the finished dock often mistook it for a bridge that had been washed out in a flood, but they knew nothing about docks, or dippers either for that matter.

The dipper's board was now gone, and he with it. Glorious silence filled the land. I had worried that the dipper might turn the dock into his own private gym, but the deck was apparently too high off the water to suit him, or perhaps he was afraid of the structure, as even some humans were.

"I miss that little bird," Bun said one morning after the dock was completed.

"Me too," I said. "Henh henh."

"I really enjoyed watching him. He always seemed so cheerful, he made me happy, too."

"Yeah yeah," I said. "What's for breakfast?"

"Before we discuss the topic of 'what's for breakfast,' " Bun replied, "I want you to promise you'll do something for me."

Old Harold Wizzel stopped by later in the morning and found me standing out in the river.

"Whatcha building?" Harold asked.

"A dipper board," I said crankily. "What does it look like?"

"How come you building a dipper board?"

"Well, if you must know, Harold, it was either this or learn how to cook."

"What's a dipper, anyway?"

The dipper never returned to use his new board. "I think you must have offended him," Bun said.

"Maybe," I said. "I certainly hope so."

My latest run-in with a bird occurred last winter. It was one of those nasty days full of wet and wind, and overcast with gloom. As I waited sullenly at my fourth stoplight in as many intersections, the faint notes of bird song penetrated my consciousness. I glared in the direction of the disturbance.

There in a stubby tree planted by the street department in its continuing effort to obstruct the view of converging drivers, a Drab Little Bird clung precariously to a wind-whipped branch, singing its heart out! I could not help but be moved by the sight. That little bird, wet, cold, and obviously miserable, had absolutely nothing to sing about, but still it sang. "Surely there is some lesson to be learned from this,'' I said to myself, ''other than the fact that this bird is either a fool or a lunatic.''

Alas, I was distracted from my reverie when the trucker behind me attempted to implode my eardrums with a blast from his air horn. In response, I thrashed wildly about the interior of my small sedan, almost impaling myself on the stick shift, for I know the keen disappointment truckers feel if the blast from their air horns doesn't prompt some such energetic display from a victim. Retrieving my composure, along with my spectacles, which had handily hung up on the rearview mirror, I deduced the reason for the trucker's impatience with me: the signal light had switched from red to green during my pondering of the lunatic bird.

Not to be outdone, the engine of my car decided to contribute to the occasion by expiring with a cough and a jerk, and then stubbornly refusing to be revived. The burly trucker, as seen through my rearview mirror, appeared on the verge of a meltdown, or so I judged from the steam issuing from around the band of his size-eight cowboy hat. Obviously, he assumed my continued delay at the green light was for the sole purpose of irritating him or even—heaven forbid!—teaching him some manners. It is this sort of innocent misunderstanding that can lead to the inconvenience of taking your nutrients through a tube in your arm. I wondered if it would help matters if I walked back and told the trucker about how I had been distracted by the little bird's singing in the rain. He might get a kick out of it. Then again, maybe not. Luckily, at that moment my engine ignited, and I spurted to safety beneath the amber glow of the caution light. While he waited for the next green light, perhaps the trucker, too, would hear the brave little nutty bird and thereby have his mood transformed to the wonderful serenity of being one with nature. But I wouldn't bet on it.

A Good Deed
Goes Wrong

Some people thought Crazy Eddie Muldoon and I were to blame for breaking Rancid Crabtree's leg. Oddly, the odorous and crotchety old woodsman himself was one of the people who thought this. He said as soon as he got off his crutches he intended to run Eddie and me down and whale the tar out of us. We weren't too worried. We figured by the time Rancid got out of the cast he would have cooled off enough to see that the accident was really his own doing and no fault of ours. But before he got off his crutches, the little incident with the bobcat occurred, generally confusing matters even more. As Crazy Eddie observed at the time, you try to do a kind deed for a person, and it just gets you into more trouble. Anyway, here are the true facts about the entire mess.

During our Christmas vacation from third grade, Eddie and

I built a toboggan run up on the mountain behind Rancid's shack. The design of our run was based on one we had seen in newsreels at the Pandora Theater the Saturday before. The two runs were almost identical, except ours was steeper and faster than the one in the newsreel, and went over and under logs and had brush on both sides of it, and at least one of the turns was much sharper, and if you didn't make that turn you would be shot off into space and sail for some time over the valley looking down at the tiny cows and cars beneath you, and this in turn might elevate your anxiety to a dangerous level. So you wanted to be sure to make that sharp curve.

We built the first part of the run on an old logging road that zigzagged down the mountain. We tramped up and down the road the distance of two switchbacks, packing down the snow into a track slightly wider than the width of our sled. The grade on the switchbacks was modest, but sufficient to build up a fair head of speed in a sled by the time it and its driver reached the curve at the end of the second switchback. Then came the good part. Instead of curving the track onto the next switchback, we funneled it over the edge of the road into an old skid trail.

The skid trail had been gouged into the mountains by old-time loggers dragging logs down it. In fact, it was so steep they probably didn't have to drag the logs but merely had to roll them into it and let them shoot to the bottom of the mountain. Erosion had cut the trail down to bare rock, which was now coated with ice, making it even better for a toboggan run. When we were building up our curved bank to funnel the track into the skid trail, Eddie slipped and nearly shot down the run with nothing but his body, and would have if he hadn't managed to grab a small tree and pull himself back up.

"Wow!" he said. "This is going to be good!"

At the bottom end, the skid trail intersected with the next switchback of the road. This was where the toboggan driver would shoot off into space if he failed to make the turn onto the switchback. Fortunately, there was a high bank on the downhill side of the road, only slightly offset from the track. The driver would have to be alert enough to steer toward the high bank, which would sweep the sled up and around and then redirect it back down onto the switchback. This was the last switchback and it provided a straightaway that, at the bottom, merged with the Sand Creek road. The straightaway was quite steep, so the toboggan driver wouldn't have to worry about his speed diminishing any when he hit this last stretch. He could then glide to a gradual stop on the Sand Creek road, which was seldom traveled during winter, and even then only by old Mrs. Swisher, who drove to church on it each Sunday. We completed the track on a Friday, and planned to make our first test run on Saturday.

The next morning, Crazy Eddie and I were dragging my sled past Rancid's shack on our way up to test our toboggan run and were arguing about who got to go down it first.

"Listen, Eddie, it's my sled!" I said.

"Yeah, that's right," he replied. "That's why you should get to be first to test the run."

"No sirree," I said. "I should be the one who gets to choose who goes first, and I choose you."

About then Rancid stuck his head out the door of his shack. "What you boys up to now?" he hollered at us. "Some kinder monkey bidness, no doubt. Ah ain't never seen no younguns what could get into more trouble than you two."

"We built a toboggan run up on the mountain, just like in the newsreel, Rancid. It's fast, too."

"Hold up a sec," he said, putting on his coat. "Ah better go check this out. You fool half-pints probably invented some new way to kill yersevs."

Half an hour later, we stood at the start of the toboggan run, all of us still puffing great clouds of vapor from the climb up the trail.

Rancid stared at the little track going down the first switchback. It didn't look nearly so impressive this morning. "Shoot," he said, chuckling. "You call this a toboggan run? Ah cain't believe Ah clumb all the way up hyar to see this piddlin' little trail in the snow. Ah must hev been outta maw mind. Gimme thet sled. The least you can do is let me ride back to the bottom of the mountain on it."

I handed over the sled. Rancid plopped down on it, sitting upright with his long legs sticking way out in front, his coat completely concealing the sled beneath him.

"It might be dangerous, Mr. Crabtree," Eddie warned.

"Dangerous!" Rancid said. "Eddie, Ah 'spect Ah never told you, but Ah used to be a professional bobsledder, jist like you see in the movies. Racin' Rancid they use to call me."

"Gee," I said. "I didn't know that." I figured that he must have been a professional bobsledder right after being a fighter pilot and before he became a big-game hunter in Africa or about the same time he was a champion prize-fighter.

"Yep," Rancid said, poking a wad of chewing tobacco into his cheek. "Now gimme a shove off."

He glided slowly away toward the first curve, gradually picking up speed. He called back to us as he went around the curve. "Ah hate to tell you this, boys, but your bobsled track ain't steep enough even to give a feller a decent ride."

We were disappointed in the professional bobsledder's assessment of our run but thought his opinion of it might improve later on. Sure enough, the next time we heard him yell was about when we thought he should hit the funnel into the skid trail:

"GOL-DAAAAAAA-A-A-A-a-a-n-n-n-n-g-g-g-g!"

"I think he liked the skid-trail section," Eddie said.

"Yeah," I said. "He sounded excited."

So that is how Rancid broke his leg. He said later he didn't know when, where, or how he broke his leg, or even that he had, because his mind was so occupied with other matters, among which was whaling the tar out of Eddie and me at the first opportunity.

The only eyewitness other than Rancid was old Mrs. Swisher, who was a little daft anyway and really couldn't be relied on for an accurate observation. "I got a little mixed up," she related, "and thinking it was Sunday instead of Saturday, I started driving to town to go to church. As always, I was especially nervous going by that dreadful Rancid Crabtree's shack, because he's in cahoots with the devil. Well, I'm driving along real careful minding my own business when all of sudden that fool Crabtree zooms right by me, just flying he was, about a foot in the air, going like the wind. I just caught a glimpse of his face, he was going so fast, and I'm sorry I did, because it had such a hideous expression on it you can't even imagine! The thought of it has kept me awake nights ever since. And he's holding this little green tree in one hand, torn right out by the roots it was. I bet the tree had something to do with one of those devilish rites of his. Well, he shot off down Sand Creek Hill, and I thought he might be laying in ambush for me up ahead, so I turned right around and went home, and it was a good thing I did, too, because then I remembered it was Saturday instead of Sunday.''

Naturally, nobody took daft old Mrs. Swisher's account seriously, although Eddie and I did recover my sled at the bottom of Sand Creek Hill, where it had shot off over the bank and landed on the frozen creek. Sprayed out in front of it was what we first thought to be blood but then discovered was nothing more interesting than tobacco juice.

A couple of Saturdays later, Eddie and I were walking along the highway pulling my sled, the runners of which were somewhat splayed out but still worked. We had been trying to come up with an idea for making amends with Rancid, when we saw a furry shape lying on the highway. Both of us had fine roadkill collections and this specimen looked exceptional.

"It's mine," I said as we rushed forward. "You got the last one."

"No sirree," Eddie said. "I remember. You got that nice flattened toad last fall and . . . Hey, what is this, anyway?"

"My gosh, it's a bobcat. Feel it. It must have just been killed. It's still warm. Look, it's got a bit of blood on its head where the car hit it, but otherwise it's in great shape. Well, I'd better take my bobcat home. Maybe I'll stuff it."

"No you won't," Eddie said. "I'm gonna take it home and stuff it."

"Hey, wait a minute," I said. "I know what. We'll give it to Rancid. He can skin it and sell the hide. Then he won't be mad at us anymore. What do you say, Eddie?"

Eddie reluctantly agreed. We loaded the bobcat on my sled and hauled it over to Rancid's shack. I pushed the door gently open and peeked inside, to make sure Rancid wasn't close enough to swat me before he saw we had brought him a gift. The old woodsman was still in bed, snoring loudly, his casted foot sticking out from under the covers and resting on a block of firewood. He had pulled a red wool stocking cap over his bare foot where it stuck out of the cast.

"Rancid's still asleep," I whispered to Eddie. "Should we wake him up?"

Crazy Eddie grinned. "Naw, he's probably all pooped out from dragging that cast around with him. Let's just carry the bobcat in and put it on the table next to his bed, so he can see it when he first wakes up. It'll be a nice surprise for him."

Eddie was very good at thinking up nice surprises for people. We carried the bobcat in and laid it down on the table next to the snoring Rancid. Eddie studied the arrangement.

"No good," he whispered. "It looks too dead." He looked around and found a box of kitchen matches. Then he took out two of the matches and used them to prop apart the big cat's lips in a pretty fair imitation of a snarl. Then he stuck the matchbox under the animal's chin so it looked as if the bobcat were holding its head up, ready to spring. Then we tiptoed out and hunkered alongside the door to await the old woodsman's awakening.

"I think he's gonna be real surprised," Eddie said.

"Yeah, me too."

Presently, Rancid stopped snoring. He muttered something in his sleep. Then he apparently banged the table with his arm, because we heard a bump and then the sound of the matchbox hitting the floor.

"Darn," Eddie whispered. "The matchbox fell out from under the bobcat's chin. The surprise is ruined now."

"Whazzat?" Rancid mumbled. "What in tarnation . . . ? GOL-DANG! GIT! GIT AWAY FROM MEEEE!"

Eddie and I chuckled.

The table crashed to the floor. A chair was flung against the wall and a block of firewood sailed out the door. All of this was accompanied by a terrible roaring and snarling and the wildest cussing I had ever heard.

"GIT BACK! GIT BACK!" Rancid yelled amid all the bangs and crashes and thumps.

Eddie looked at me. "I didn't think he'd be this surprised."

"No fooling," I said nervously. "Maybe we'd better leave right now. We can tell him later about our present for him, when he isn't so surprised."

At that moment there was a furious rattling of crutches and Rancid burst out of the cabin, shot across the yard and into his privy, slamming the door shut behind him.

Eddie and I were so startled we couldn't move. Then the bobcat walked out the door, chewing on a matchstick. It gave us a contemptuous glance and went off up the mountain shaking its head, either because it had a headache or because it couldn't believe what it had just witnessed.

Rancid opened the privy door a crack and watched the bobcat until it disappeared in the woods. Then he saw us. Crazy Eddie and I started toward home.

"You ever seen Rancid move that fast before?" Eddie asked.

"Nope," I said, glancing back over my shoulder. "'Specially not on crutches."

"Didn't even use his legs," Eddie said, with a touch of awe. "Had those ol' crutches whippin' around like spokes on a wheel. Do you think he was ever an acrobat in a circus?"

"Probably."

"I see he don't sleep in pajamas neither," Eddie said, puffing clouds of vapor into the icy air.

"Yeah," I said, panting my own clouds of vapor. "He probably will after this, though."

We passed daft old Mrs. Swisher's car askew on the road below Rancid's shack. She was staring vacantly at us, her mouth hanging open.

"It's Saturday, Mrs. Swisher," Eddie yelled as we sped past. "Sunday ain't till tomorrow."

She didn't reply. But I could tell she was going to have trouble getting to sleep again that night. It isn't often you see a naked man on crutches with a red stocking cap on his foot chase two boys through the snow on a cold winter morning. What was even stranger, the crippled old woodsman kept gaining on us.

The Fishing Box

A fishing box, I should explain right off, is not the same as a tackle box. Unfishing spouses often confuse the two, as in "How many fishing boxes do you need, anyway?" (You need an infinite number of tackle boxes, but that's beside the point.) A fishing box, then, is simply a container, usually of cardboard, into which you dump odd fishing stuff that doesn't qualify for space in your tackle boxes. It serves as a repository for things you might find a use for someday, although probably not in this century. It also serves to tidy up the space you use for storing and working on your tackle, whether den, shop, garage, living room, or bedroom. Some fishermen prefer simply to use the floor instead of a fishing box. That is fine, too, but the tackle should be kicked into neat little piles, with walking space between them. This bit of tidiness takes some extra effort, but your thoughtfulness will be much appreciated by your spouse, at least for the brief period she remains in residence.

What size fishing box do you need? They come in all sizes, ranging from empty cigar boxes to major-household-appliance boxes. If you are eight years old and just getting started with your collection of fishing tackle, there is no point in rushing out and buying a major household appliance just to start big, so I recommend to youngsters that they start small, with a cigar box, and, when it is full, move up to a shoe box. Warning: do not store leftover worms in these boxes. They will spoil quickly and attract flies, ants, and, much more threatening, mothers. At this point in your young life, you may regard the contents of the box as treasures rather than junk, and therefore may be horrified to discover your fishing box missing. You will naturally assume it has been stolen, but chances are it has merely been misplaced. Tip: check the garbage can first. This problem can be avoided by not placing leftover worms in the box; instead, store them where they belong—in the refrigerator. Empty cottage-cheese containers are excellent for this purpose, and often result in a few good laughs, although probably not in the near future. Once you reach adulthood, or about the time your mother laughs about the cottage-cheese container for the first time, you will no longer regard the contents of your fishing box as precious treasures, but will come to consider most items as the oddball junk they really are. Later in this article, I will set forth the proper procedure for cleaning out the fishing box and selecting only those few objects worth keeping. Those old reels gunked up with sand and rust, for example, may someday be worth a lot of money as antiques. (Then again, they may only be old reels gunked up with sand and rust. But who knows?)

For the adult angler, any cardboard container with six or eight cubic feet of space will serve nicely for a fishing box, as long as the opening on top is at least the size of a regulation basketball hoop. When one fishing box is full, simply start another one. Add boxes as you need them, until you are ready for a new major household appliance.

What kinds of things are typically dumped in the fishing box? Old "hot" lures are commonly assigned to it. By "old" I mean those five-dollar lures you bought last year, because they were the hot lures then. The fish, of course, aren't taking those hot lures now. No creature is more fickle or fashion conscious than a fish: each year it requires a new look in lures. Fish who bite on last year's hot lures become the target of ridicule in their schools, often being called names like "nerd" or, much harsher, "fish stick." I suggest consigning all of last year's hot lures to the fishing box, preferably with jump hook shots from across the room, a common method employed by experienced anglers.

Another item relegated to the fishing box is the single stray of almost anything, such as the one hook or plastic worm that shows up on your workbench after you've put everything else away. You're ready to head in and watch your favorite TV show when you hear a small voice from the top of the workbench: "What about me?" You look down and there is one stray purple plastic worm. Are you going to sort through your tackle boxes looking for the one with the purple plastic worm compartment? Of course not. What you do is grasp the worm by the tail, leap straight up, and whip it over your head in a high, arcing hook shot toward the fishing box. Two points! You smile and go watch your show.

Objects consigned to the fishing box include, among other

things, jelled masses of stuff, which happen to contain good hooks, spinners, sinkers, and other items you can't quite bring yourself to discard with the glob. I do not know much about these globs, except that they appear from time to time in my tackle boxes, particularly those containing tubes and packages of synthetic bait, which may explain the pungent odor. (Check garbage can for missing tackle boxes again.) Sometimes the globs consist of half-melted plastic worms, which can be pretty darn gross, especially with those wiggly tails extruding lifelike from the solidified goo. By the way, never leave these half-melted plastic-worm globs where your wife might come across them unexpectedly, such as in the bottom of her purse. This happened once at our house, while my wife was groping in her purse for car keys just prior to rushing off late for a hair appointment. Took all the curl out of her hair and cost me fifty bucks for a new permanent, when I could have gotten by with a mere trim. Took some of the curl out of my hair, too, particularly when our mailman threatened to sue me, as though it were my fault he scattered letters halfway down the block. It is best simply to gouge the globs out of the tackle box with a putty knife, flick them at the fishing box, and be done with them.

Also destined for the fishing box are terminally tangled clusters of lures, in which each barb of each treble hook has mysteriously inserted itself through the eye or tiny split ring of another treble hook, but in such a way that each lure is attached to twelve other lures. The mystery resides in the fact that if you were to take two lures and deliberately jiggle them about for a week you would never be able to get one barb to slip through a single eye or split ring on the other lure. But topple a tackle box off a boat seat just once and all those little barbs and tiny hook eyes converge on one another. Some of them have to wait in line while others go through the complicated gyrations required to get properly connected. The latecomer barbs sometimes find all the eyes and split rings taken, so they have to crowd in with other barbs. One big hook is probably in charge of the activities, yelling out in a wiry voice, "I have room for one more barb in a treble-hook eye over here! Two more barbs can crowd into that split ring over there! Snap it up, folks, because old Joe is going to open this tackle box any second now. Everybody get ready to yell 'Surprise!' "

All the fantastic bargains in tackle you picked out of the discount basket at the sporting-goods store because the price was just too good to resist are also fishing-box bound. Some anglers actually go to the trouble of removing the individual items from the plastic-bubble packages before chucking the bargains into the fishing box. I personally find it more efficient to hook-shot them in as a group, while they are still in the sack from the store. Unbelievable as it may seem, I once knew a man who claimed actually to have caught a fish on one of these bargains from the discount basket, but he was an expert fisherman who knew how to select just the right lure for the right occasion, how to cast it into the perfect spot, how to retrieve it at just the proper speed and depth, and how to lie with a straight face.

All fishing gifts given to you by friends and relatives who regard themselves as having a wonderful sense of humor qualify as prime candidates for the fishing box. It is only polite to open these gifts and respond good-naturedly to the little joke: "Oh, Aunt Jane, you are such a comic! Where did you ever find a fish tie? A rainbow trout, isn't it? This is wonderful! Please excuse me while I go put this away before it gets smudged or wrinkled." Two points!

Many newfangled inventions end up in the fishing box, such as the power fish-scaler that went berserk and scaled half a bass, three of your fingers, a patch of lawn, and the neighbors' cat. Then there are several latest models of electronic fish-finders that are no longer the latest models. These include the ultimate fish-finder, which was ultimate for only three months.

My fishing box contains several dozen survey forms—folded into paper airplanes—asking four hundred questions ranging from how, where, and why I bought a product to how much money I earn, as though it's any of their business. (You'd think they'd be satisfied simply with my having bought their product, but no, they have to pry into my personal life as well. If I ever filled out and mailed one of these forms, the company officers would probably sit around joking and laughing about how much money I earn.)

To-do lists—folded into paper airplanes—intended to bring some order to your fishing tackle are common fishing-box residents. Item number eighty-seven on a list is "Clean out fishing box and discard all useless items." This is a chore that really should be attended to, at least once every four or five years. It is through the process of "cleaning out" that the true function of the fishing box becomes evident, namely the careful selection of the few items that seem to have intrinsic value and the trash-canning of the obvious junk.

The procedure for cleaning out the fishing box, as practiced by the mature fisherman, is simply to turn the box upside down and dump the contents on the floor. He carefully sorts through the items by nudging them about with the toe of his shoe. He stares contemplatively at the stuff. He strolls down memory lane over the sight of his old slick-soled wading shoes that teamed up with a rock to give him a memorable compound fracture of the rear end. And there are the tatters of the landing net with which he landed his first respectable fish, something over nine inches as he recalls. And by golly if that isn't the old wicker creel with the overlooked perch permanently blended into the wicker. Why, he thinks, this is a regular hoard of . . . of . . . treasure! It's *all* treasure! So he shovels it all back into the fishing box. When he's finished "cleaning out," he heads in to watch his favorite TV program. But then softly, almost imperceptibly, he hears a tiny voice from the floor: "What about me?" Well, here's about you. Leap. Hook shot. Two points!

Social Skills

One thing I can't abide in an outdoorsman is whining. That's why my persnickety next-door neighbor Al Finley, the city councilperson, gets on my nerves so much. Some little thing will go wrong, and Al has to whine about it. For several years now, Retch Sweeney and I have been trying to teach hunting to Finley. Last week, on a pheasant hunt, we concentrated on social skills. Al whined all day long.

"How come I always have to be the one to go up to the farmhouse and ask the farmer permission to hunt on his land?" Finley whined.

"Because you need the practice, that's why," Retch snapped.

"That's absolutely right," I said. "And if you had paid attention to our instructions on how to make friends with farmers' dogs, this never would have happened. Now you take this little mutt here—pay attention, Al! Notice how he is growling at me. First, I start by smiling at him and speaking softly. Easy, little fella, don't be afraid. Nice doggie. Okay, now I reach out very carefully and scratch him behind the ears. Hey, you like that, don't you, pooch? See, he's starting to wag his tail, always a good sign. He's rolling his big brown eyes up at me, just like I'm his long-lost friend. Now he's relaxing his jaws, and there we go, I have him unclamped from your rear end, Finley.''

"About time, too," Finley whined. "You should have let me slam the little beast's head in the car door the way I wanted to.''

"Cripes!" Retch said. "That's why we're trying to teach you some social skills, Finley. Farmers never let you hunt after you've slammed their dog's head in a car door.''

"Why, you silly elbow. . . . " Finley muttered.

"Okay, calm down, you two," I said. "Let's analyze what happened here. First of all, Al, you were told not to run if a dog threatened you. And you ran. That's the worst thing you can do. It merely excites the dog to attack. This little fella got so excited he leaped up and snapped on to your rear. Okay, I'll admit that Retch and I shouldn't have laughed, but when you cleared the picket fence with that little dog flapping behind you . . ." Here I tried unsuccessfully to suppress an outburst of mirth.

"Yeah, yeah," Finley said. "Very funny! Well, at the next farm one of you elbows can go up to the farmhouse and ask permission and show me how it's done.''

The next farm looked like an excellent prospect for hunting, particularly since we had to stop the car while a huge herd of pheasants crossed the road and disappeared into one of the overgrown fields. The farm was not typical of the area, where most of the places were kept in tip-top condition. Here the fields were full of weeds, the fence posts askew or rotted off, the buildings in need of paint. Pieces of farm machinery and old cars were scattered about in various stages of disintegration. The farmhouse itself had a brooding, threatening aspect to it, with the paint peeling from the warped siding, withered brown vines slithering up over the front porch, and here and there a broken window patched with a piece of cardboard.

Retch stopped the car well back on the driveway and the three of us stared silently at the house for a few minutes. "Well," I said to Finley, "here is where you pass or fail the final exam on hunting social skills. Walk on up there and get us permission to hunt."

"Are you out of your mind?" Finley yelped. "Didn't you see that sign back there, 'Trespassers will be shot, ground up, and fed to the hogs'?"

"That just goes to show the farmer has a sense of humor," Retch said. "Now get a move on."

"No!"

"Want to walk home?"

"Stop it, you two," I said. "I'll tell you what, Al. I'll walk up to the house with you. But you have to knock on the door and do all the talking."

Finley reluctantly agreed. As we were getting out of the car, Retch glanced nervously around and said, "Say, I'll tell you what. While you fellas are getting permission, I'll zip back to that little town and get us some stuff for lunch. How does that sound?"

Before I could tell him how that sounded, he had put the car in reverse and shot back up the driveway.

"Great!" Finley whined. "Just great! Now if a dog takes after us, we'll have to run all the way back to town to slam its head in a car door!"

"For gosh sakes," I said. "How many times do I have to tell you? Never run from a dog!"

As we walked up the driveway toward the house, Finley said, "Speaking of d-dogs, look at the size of that doghouse over there."

"Don't be silly," I said. "That's not a doghouse. It's way too big."

"Then why is the name 'Fido' painted over the door?"

"I don't know. Maybe they have a Shetland pony they call Fido, who knows? But just look at the size of the chain hooked to the house. Obviously, a dog would have to be the size of a horse to need a chain like that. There doesn't seem to be a dog of any kind around here, anyway. Otherwise, it would be out here barking at us by now."

"Maybe it's setting a trap for us," Finley said. "Luring us in close so he can jump us."

Finley was starting to make me nervous with his whining about dogs. "Would you stop it?" I said, glancing about.

I sized up the situation. The back door looked like the best bet to knock on. The entryway was off an enclosed carport, which, unfortunately, did not contain a vehicle. That's usually a bad sign, an indication that no one is home. I told Finley to knock on the door anyway, which he did. No one was home. Disappointed, we turned to leave, but stopped so abruptly our shoes made little squeaking sounds on the concrete floor. Then Finley and I made little squeaking sounds with our mouths. A massive black beast with doglike features was slowly advancing toward the entrance of the carport. Its lips were curled back over fangs the size of railroad spikes. Great rumbling growls emerged from its dark interior, serious, no-nonsense growls, the self-righteous growls of a dog that knows it has caught two burglars on the property and is now going to redeem itself with its master for all its past mischief by tearing the intruders to shreds. From the size and wrath of the beast, I doubted there would be enough left of us even to serve to the hogs as an appetizer.

I realized instantly the futility of trying to reason with the enraged creature. What I needed was a diversion. Suddenly, one leaped to mind.

"Run, Finley, run!" I whispered to him. "It's your only chance."

Finley, still making the little squeaking sounds, shook his head. Why he picked this moment to start following my previous instructions about dogs I don't know, but I was a good deal peeved at him. The black monster backed us slowly toward the rear of the carport, trying to herd us both into a single corner, possibly with the intention of dispatching the two of us more efficiently. As I eased backward, trying as best I could to shield myself with what was at hand, namely Finley, I reached out and tried the doorknob of the house. Unlocked! I opened the door, leaped inside, and started to gesture for Finley to follow, but he was already standing in the middle of the kitchen, thus explaining the blur that had passed me a second before. I slammed the door, just as the dog sprang at it. The force of the impact loosened the screws in the hinges, but the door held, now bent slightly inward. The dog, obviously disappointed, set himself the task of gnawing his way through the door.

While Finley stood in the middle of the kitchen and shook, I strode calmly back and forth trying to figure a way out of our predicament. Then I noticed I was eating a peach. I hadn't been eating a peach when we entered the house, and now I was eating a peach. How odd. I glanced at the kitchen table and there were four peaches in a bowl. I had absent-mindedly snatched up a peach and started eating it, such was my power of concentration at that moment. With some amusement, I started to call Finley's attention to this, only to discover that he was staring at me in gaping horror.

"You're eating a peach!" he cried, stating the obvious. "Not only do you break and enter, you eat the farmer's food besides! We're going to do time for this!"

"Would you stop the whining, Finley?" I said. "It's get-ting on my nerves. If the farmer comes home before we get out of here, we'll just explain the situation to him. I'm sure he'll understand." I sucked the peach pit clean and stuck it in my pocket. No point in leaving evidence lying about, just in case the police should become involved.

"Understand!" Finley said. "You think when that farmer steps through the door of this house and sees two complete strangers standing in his kitchen, he's going to give you time for an explanation?"

"I suppose you have a better idea."

"We'll hide!"

"Nonsense," I replied. "I'm sure the farmer will respond with good humor to my explanation of the incident. Indeed, I wouldn't be a bit surprised if it doesn't give him a good chuckle."

At that moment we heard a car coming up the driveway. I peeked through the curtain. A sedan was pulling into the carport. It contained a beefish man, a hulking teenage boy, and a large, husky woman. All were scowling and yelling back and forth at each other. They got out of the car. I rehearsed my little speech explaining the oddity that Finley and I happened to be standing in their kitchen.

"What's that crazy dog doing?" the man roared. "Stop that, Fido! Luther, grab that fool dog and go chain him up. First I get two flat tires and run out of gas, and then I come home and find my dog eating my house! What next! One more thing goes wrong today I'm gonna fly off the handle!"

I grabbed Finley by the arm and thrust him toward the living room. "I just came up with a better idea, Al. Hide!"

We rushed into the living room and up a flight of stairs. Finley, his knees buckling from fright, dodged through a door that turned out to be a bathroom. I tried to tell him that a bathroom was a terrible place to hide from a family that had just returned from a trip to town, but it was too late. Someone was tromping angrily up the stairs. I ducked into a hall closet, leaving the door open a crack so I could peek out. The farmer's husky wife came striding down the hall. She opened the bathroom door, went in, and closed the door behind her. I braced myself for the scream. I thought it possible the farmer's wife might scream, too, but it seemed unlikely. Probably she would just hurl Finley through the closed door and then come out and stomp him. Perhaps while she was stomping him, I could make a break for it. Finley might yet serve as a diversion.

Presently, however, the woman came out of the bathroom and went off downstairs. A few seconds later, Finley stuck his head out the door and looked up and down the hall. He had a crazed look on his face.

While the coast was clear, I jumped out of the closet and rushed over to Finley.

"How . . . ?" I started to ask.

"Hid in the shower," he said, his hushed voice shrill

from the stress of the past few moments. "Now I'm sure we're going to do time!"

Finley sank into what appeared to be near paralysis, drool dribbling disgustingly from the corner of his quivering lips. I grabbed him by the shirtfront and dragged him after me into a bedroom, where I opened a window and pushed him out. Finley bounced onto the slanted carport roof, slid down to the edge, and dropped unharmed to the ground. I made a mental note to chastise him later for dragging his fingernails on the metal roof, which had produced a hideous screeching similar to the nerve-fraying sound we boys once scratched out on schoolroom chalkboards. Why Finley would choose a time like that for such juvenile behavior, I can't say, but I found it not the least bit amusing.

Having ascertained that the escape route was safe enough and not likely to cause serious injury, I followed Finley to the ground. He was sitting there in a befuddled state, which was a good deal more pleasant to me than his constant whining. I pulled him to his feet, dusted him off, and dragged him after me toward the driveway. As soon as we stepped around the corner, however, Fido set up a maniacal barking. A few seconds later, the farmer bounded out of the house.

"What the . . . ?" he said, even as his biceps bulged menacingly, by which I mean stretching his shirt cuffs halfway up to his elbows.

"Good day, sir," I said. "Fine place you have here. And an excellent watchdog, too, I might add. Big fellow, isn't he? Probably good with children, if I don't miss my guess. But to the point, sir. I was wondering if you might be so kind as to let us hunt on your property."

"Shucks, mister, I don't mind at all," he replied, smiling.

"Just shut the gates after yourselves. Good luck. Stop by on your way out. The wife's gonna bake a peach pie. Be pleased if you stopped in for some pie and a cup of coffee."

"We'd be delighted," I said.

At that moment, the farmer's wife screamed from the kitchen. "Luther, you rotten kid, you ate one of the peaches I was saving for a pie!"

"Did not, Ma!" the boy's voice shouted back.

"Luther, don't lie to you ma!" the farmer bellowed toward the house. He grinned at Finley and me. "Ain't safe to leave food around that kid. Sucks up grub like a gol-durn vacuum cleaner."

I grinned back. "Boys will be boys, I guess."

Retch arrived back just then. I thanked the farmer for his generosity and walked over to the car, dragging Finley along by his shirtfront.

"How'd it go?" Retch asked.

"Fine," I said. "We can hunt."

"Great," Retch said. "What's wrong with Finley?"

"Nothing that a little more practice in the social skills of hunting won't cure," I said.

"But he's so pale and shaky," Retch said. "He ain't even whining."

"Don't worry," I said. "He'll get around to it."

The Clown

I admit it: my sense of humor is a bit weird. It's caused me some trouble over the years. For example, the only time I ever got sent to the principal's office at Delmore Blight Junior High was because I laughed in the wrong place at the wrong time—Miss Bindle's math class.

They don't make teachers like Miss Bindle anymore. At least, I hope they don't. She was tiny, scrawny, and fierce, with an eighty-year-old face and twenty-year-old red hair. Her wrinkles were permanently fused into a frown beneath the glowing halo of frizzy hair. Miss Bindle was the Jesse James of sarcasm: she could quick-draw a sarcastic remark and drill you between the eyes with it at thirty paces. She once hit Mort Simmons with a slug of sarcasm that spun him around half out of his desk. Then she walked over and coolly finished him off with two shots to the head. Mort recovered, but he was never the same afterward. His was a sad case.

Mort had always been dumb. The reason Miss Bindle drilled him was that he had been sneaking a look at one of my answers during a test, that's how dumb he was, or so Miss Bindle remarked, catching me with a ricochet from her shot at Mort. She never coddled us dumb kids, as did some of the kinder, more merciful teachers. She made us learn the same stuff as the smart kids. A few teachers took pity on us and let us relax in the cozy vacuum of our dumbness, but Miss Bindle forced us to learn everything the smart kids did, even though it took us three times as long. Everybody hated her for it, even the smart kids, who were cheated out of the satisfaction of knowing more than the dumb ones. Anybody could see that wasn't fair.

But I started to tell about Mort. He couldn't do arithmetic without counting on his fingers. Miss Bindle said she didn't care what parts of his anatomy he had to count on, he was going to learn just as much math as anybody else. Mort did, too, but it was a terrible strain on him, dumb as he was. When we got to multiplying and dividing fractions his fingers moved so fast he had to keep a glass of ice water on his desk to cool them off. It was a good thing we didn't do algebra in seventh grade, because somebody would have had to stand next to Mort with a fire extinguisher.

It is my understanding that modern educational theory dismisses the use of fear as a means of inducing learning in adolescents. Educators now take a more civilized approach and try to make learning an enjoyable experience. I agree with that. I know that all my children enjoyed school much more than I did. On the other hand, none of them knows how to multiply and divide fractions. I suppose that's part of the trade-off.

Fear was Miss Bindle's one and only motivator. It was as though she had done her teacher training at Marine boot camp. She would stick her face an inch from yours and, snarling and snapping, rearrange the molecules of your brain to suit her fancy. It was clearly evident to the person whose brain molecules were being rearranged that breath mints either hadn't been invented or hadn't come in a flavor pleasing to Miss Bindle. The oral hygiene of an executioner, however, is scarcely a matter of great concern to the potential victim.

Miss Bindle preferred psychological violence—whipping your psyche into a pink froth—to physical violence. Physical violence was direct and straightforward, something all of us youngsters thoroughly understood. There was no mystery to it. Given a choice, we would have taken the teacher's physical violence, which consisted of snatching the culprit by the hair and dragging him off to the principal's office. As I say, Miss Bindle was extremely short, only about half the size of some of the larger boys. When Miss Bindle grabbed them by the hair and took off for the office, they had to trail along behind her in a bent-over posture, which didn't do a lot for the macho image of some of the guys, particularly if they were saying, "Ow ow ow," as they went out the door. On the other hand, if they had stood erect, in order to depart from the room in a dignified fashion, Miss Bindle would have dangled from their hair, her feet swinging a good six inches off the floor. It was a no-win situation, and wisdom dictated the less painful of the two modes of being escorted to the office. In contrast to Miss Bindle, other teachers merely pointed toward the door and ordered, "Go to the office!" This method allowed the typical louts, some of whom were near voting age, to leave the room swaggering and sneering. No lout ever left Miss Bindle's room swaggering and sneering.

I was a fairly timid fellow, and took great care never to attract the wrath of Miss Bindle. I studied ways to make myself invisible in her class, with such success that a couple of times she marked me absent when I was there. Pitiful victims were snatched from their desks on all sides of me, but month after month I escaped unsnatched, making myself increasingly invisible, until finally there were only a few weeks left of my seventh-grade sentence. I thought I was going to make it safely through to the end of the school year, but I hadn't taken into account my weird sense of humor—or my friend Slick.

Clifford Slick was the class clown. Ol' Slick felt his purpose in life was to make people laugh, and he was pretty good at it. Everybody liked Slick. We would gather around him during lunch hour to watch his routines and laugh ourselves sick. He did a wonderful impression of Miss Bindle snatching a kid by the hair and dragging him off. He did both parts alternately, the kid and Miss Bindle, and it was hilarious. One of the reasons Slick got the routine down so well was that he got snatched about once a week. It was as though he had researched the act. He knew every little nuance of a snatching, and how to exaggerate it just enough to turn the horror into humor. It was a gift.

One day before school, I made the mistake of bragging to Slick that I was going to make it all the way through the year without getting snatched by Miss Bindle. Slick was concentrating on combing his hair into a weird shape. His father had shot a bear, and Slick had come into a quantity of bear grease. He slathered a copious amount of bear grease on his hair, and was delighted to see that he could now comb it into any shape he wanted. He combed it flat down against his skull, so that it looked as though he were wearing a shiny, tight leather helmet.

"How's that look?" he asked me. "Funny?"

I grinned. "Yeah, pretty funny, Cliff. I like the one best, though, where you comb it straight out from your forehead. It looks like a duck bill. Ha!"

"Okay, good," he said. "I'll go with that. Should get some laughs. Now what was that you were saying?"

"I said I've never been snatched by Miss Bindle. I'm going to make it all the way through the year without getting snatched."

Slick turned a malevolent smile on me. "No you ain't. Today you're going to bust out laughing right in old Bindle's class!"

"Not a chance!" The mere thought of bursting out laughing in Miss Bindle's class would totally paralyze my entire laughing apparatus. It was like having a fail-safe mechanism.

"You'll laugh," Slick said. "I'll make you laugh."

I shook my head. "No way."

In the whole hundred or so years that Miss Bindle had taught, I was reasonably sure that not so much as a snicker had ever been heard in her class, let alone a laugh. It was absolutely insane for Slick to think that I, a profoundly fearful and insecure person, would achieve fame as the one kid ever to burst out laughing within snatching range of Miss Bindle.

As soon as Miss Bindle's back was turned to scratch some fractions on the blackboard, Slick went into his routine. He took a dainty sip from his ink bottle, and then made a terrible face. His greasy duck-bill hair contributed considerably to the comedy. I felt a laugh coming on, but easily strangled it. Slick looked disappointed. Then he stuck two yellow pencils up his nose, his impression of a walrus. I felt a major laugh inflating inside me. Slick next imitated a walrus tak-

ing a dainty sip of tea. That almost got me, but the laugh
exploded deep in my interior with a muffled *whump!* Suspic-
ious, Olga Bonemarrow, in the next row, glared at me.
Feeling as though I had suffered major internal injuries, I
wiped some tears from my eyes. Slick took this as an en-
couraging sign and pulled out all the stops. He was doing
his duck-bill walrus daintily sipping tea while wiggling its
ears when Miss Bindle turned to face the class.

"Clifford!" she roared, hurtling down the aisle like a tiny,
ancient, redheaded dreadnought. Slick's ears ceased to wiggle; the pencils in his nose quivered; a bit of inky drool
dribbled from his gaping mouth. He clenched his eyes in
preparation for a major-league snatching. Miss Bindle
grabbed at his hair and headed off down the aisle, obviously
expecting Slick to be firmly in tow. But Slick was still seated
at his desk, eyes clenched, pencils up nose. Miss Bindle
rushed back and made another pass at his hair, but again
her hand slipped off. She snatched again and again, with
even less effect. Apparently, it was the first time she had
ever encountered bear-greased hair on one of her snatchees.

All the while, Slick sat there numbly, the yellow pencils
poking out of his nose and a terrible expression on his face.
Maybe it was Slick's expression that got to me, or maybe it
was the way the teacher stared down at her greasy palms,
her eyes full of rage and disgust and incomprehension. Whatever the trigger, it bypassed the fail-safe mechanism. My
wild, booming laugh detonated like a bomb in the frozen
silence of the room. I could scarcely believe it was my own
laugh. I hoped it might be Mort's: only he might possibly
be stupid enough to laugh in Miss Bindle's math class. But
no, the laugh, now diminishing from a roar into a sort of
breathless squealing, was none other than my own. I had

been betrayed by my weird sense of humor! By Clifford
Slick and his bear grease! And yes, even by Miss Bindle!
As I writhed in an agony of mirth, half hilarity and half
terror, I could feel Miss Bindle's stiletto eyes piercing my
living—for the moment—flesh. My stunned classmates failed
to find my laughter infectious. He who laughed in Miss
Bindle's class laughed alone.

And then it happened. "Clifford! Pat!" snarled Miss Bindle. "Go to the office!" She pointed the way with a finger
shiny with bear grease.

I left the classroom erect and dignified. Cliff went out the
door sideways, doing his comical little vaudeville dance. It
didn't get a laugh.

After the principal, Mr. Wiggens, gave us his bored lec-
ture on the importance of discipline in a learning environ-
ment, he ordered us back to class. As I was passing the
entrance of the cloakroom, I heard strange sounds emanat-
ing from the far end. A quick glance revealed that it was
Miss Bindle. At first I thought she was crying, possibly over
the disappointment of failing to snatch Cliff's and my hair.
But no! She was laughing! Cackling, actually, quietly and
to herself. It struck me that Miss Bindle had a weird sense
of humor, too.

A Good Night's Sleep

Hunters and anglers naturally prefer to carry their own sleeping accommodations right along with them in the form of sleeping bags and tents, campers, or trailers. Sometimes, however, it becomes necessary to seek out commercial lodging, a circumstance that almost always proves to be traumatic. My experience, though, has been that hotel and motel managers greatly exaggerate their traumas. I can accept the screaming and swearing, but the weeping is a bit much.

I recall the time Retch Sweeney, Clifford Gritts, and I flipped our raft while steelheading on the Tushwallop River. We made it to shore with most of our gear, but the raft floated off down the river and we had to pursue it for nearly an hour before we caught up with it. Laughing as we leaped logs and plowed through brush, we had a great time, even though Clifford did get a nasty gash over one eye when a branch hit him. He tied a grungy old bandanna around his head to sop up the blood and keep it from getting in his eye. One of my pant legs hooked on a knot and tore so badly above the knee that I just ripped it the rest of the way off. Retch Sweeney did a nose dive into the middle of what appeared to be a hog wallow, although there were no pigs about. The mosquitoes and gnats had probably carried them off. Our faces were smeared with the remains of various bloodsucking insects we had slapped to death. Obviously shaken by the viciousness of our assault on their legions, some of the smarter insects took cover in our beards and hair, from which they fought a guerrilla war. Finally, we caught up with the raft, hauled it to shore, and floated the rest of the way down to where we had parked the car.

"Whew!" Retch gasped as we tied the raft onto the top of the car. "I must be gettin' old. These little fishing trips are startin' to wear me out."

"Gee," Clifford said. "Maybe you better see a doctor. A little fishin' shouldn't tire a man."

"Yeah," I put in. "If something out of the ordinary had happened and we'd had some strenuous exercise, why, I could understand your being a bit tired. But, my gosh, Retch, a simple little float trip down the river! Clifford's right. You'd better see a doctor."

"Maybe I will," Retch said. "Maybe I will."

"And another thing," I said, "we're not gonna spend the night out in this rain, not with you dying and all. We'll get a room at that resort hotel down the road—what was it called?"

"The Cutie Pooh Resort," Clifford said, trying to squeeze some guerrillas out of his beard.

Retch didn't object, so we got in the car and drove back

to the highway without experiencing difficulty, except for getting stuck in a muddy creek bed. Retch barely had enough strength left to lift the rear end of the car while Clifford stuck some rocks and logs under the tires. The only mishap occurred when the bumper slipped out of Retch's hands and somehow popped all the buttons of his shirt, exposing the rather vulgar tattoo that had mysteriously appeared on his chest during a delightful evening we had spent in a South American seaport with a group of local literati, discussing the cultural influences on the literary works of Gabriel García Marquez. Luckily, the inscription on the tattoo was in Spanish and could be understood only by persons fluent in that language. The one explanation we ever came up with for the appearance of the tattoo was that it resulted from the curse of a man who may have been an Indian witch doctor disguised as a German tourist. Retch might unintentionally have offended the witch doctor by using him as a shield while we fought our way to the exit, the locals having taken exception to some of our critical assessments. Retch's wife said she had some trouble swallowing that theory, but then she's had no experience with witch doctors.

"That does it," I said to Retch when we got to the highway. "You're going to get a physical checkup first thing after this fishing trip. I can understand your letting a car slip out of your hands and dropping it, but not a compact, for gosh sakes."

"I know, I know!" Retch moaned. "I feel weak as a baby."

We headed down the road toward the resort, but before we had gone far, we passed the Old Country Village Antique Shop.

"Stop the car!" shouted Clifford. "Did you see what I

just saw? That antique store had a moose-head mount in
the window. I've got to have it for my den wall." He rushed
in and bought the ratty old thing and stuffed it into the
backseat with the dying Retch and the rest of our gear.

As the three of us trooped into the lobby of the Cutie
Pooh Resort, I was struck by the somber quiet and sterile
atmosphere of the place. It seemed more like a rest home
than a resort hotel, as it proclaimed itself to be. I might
have been mistaken, but my impression was that the guests
in the lobby looked upon us with a good deal of interest,
peering up from their bridge games and dominoes. I guess
that is what is meant by resort hotel—you have to resort to
inane activities to stave off the boredom.

The reception desk was unattended. Clifford pounded the
bell a few times. When that effort failed to produce a clerk,
I shouted, "Anybody home here?" Still no response. At
that moment Retch noticed the shiny black tips of two shoes
protruding from a shallow inset in a side wall, the wearer
of the shoes apparently having flattened himself into the de-
pression in an unsuccessful effort to conceal himself, for what
purpose I could not imagine.

"Hey, you with the shiny shoes," Retch yelled. "How
about a little service here?"

The desk clerk then emerged and confronted us with a
shaky grin that scarcely made an indent on his overall expression of disdain.

"Yessss?" he said, peering at us over the top of his spectacles.

"We'd like a room," I said, wincing as I leaned down
for some frenzied scratching of a few hundred mosquito bites
on the extremity from which half my pant leg had been torn.

"Sorry, we're all filled up."

"Don't give us that!" Clifford said, tweaking him on his carnation. "We have a dying man here and . . ."

At that moment Clifford began to emit absolutely horrible sounds, finally communicating through wild gestures that one of the guerrillas in his mustache had charged up a nostril with bayonet fixed.

"Quick!" I ordered Retch. "Slap him on the back of the head!"

Retch immediately obeyed and gave Clifford a clout that buckled his knees and sent the guerrilla hurtling out into space toward the startled clerk.

"Not with the steelhead!" I shouted at Retch, who was holding the twelve-pounder by the tail in preparation for giving Clifford's head another whack. "You'll bruise its flesh!"

"I'd bruise *Retch's* flesh if he wasn't already terminally ill!" roared Clifford. They got into a little shoving match.

By now the other guests in the lobby had clustered together and retreated to a far corner. They seemed rather a pitiful lot, and I wondered vaguely if they hadn't possibly come to the resort for treatment of a nervous condition.

"Please! Please, gentlemen!" pleaded the desk clerk, who seemed to have the same nervous affliction as his guests. "We don't allow rowdy behavior!"

"That's good," I replied, "because we have a seriously ill man here and he needs a good night's rest and some peace and quiet. If you have any rowdies show up, just give us a call and we'll deal with them in short order. Speaking of short order, we'd like a little grub sent up to our room."

"I told you, there is no . . . Oh, all right, we do have a room." He scribbled the room rate on a card for me to sign.

I stared at the rate card in amazement. Then I realized

the rate indicated was merely the clerk's little joke, a bit of absurdity to put us at ease.

"Hey, you're not so bad after all," I told him. "That's the funniest thing I've seen all day, you pretending that we want to buy the whole establishment instead of just renting a room for the night."

The clerk focused his attention on Retch, as though becoming aware of him for the first time. "What on earth is that?" he asked, wrinkling up his nose, an expression that caused me to mistake the intent of his question.

"We think it's pig," I replied. "It might possibly have been a bear wallow he fell into, but my general impression after spending an hour with him in a warm car is that it's pig. What's your guess?"

The clerk shuddered visibly. "I was referring not to the odor but to that rather ghastly tattoo on his chest."

"Oh," I said. "That's a real dilly of a tattoo, isn't it? My sick friend here is the only person I know with an X-rated chest. You don't read Spanish, I take it."

"No."

"Good."

After handing the steelhead to the clerk and giving him instructions for its proper care as well as a few tips on how to remove fish scales from a dark suit, we hauled some of our gear in from the car and packed it into the elevator. One of the other passengers in the elevator seemed a bit crabby and expressed his dissatisfaction with having to share an elevator with us and our gear. I apologized for the slight inconvenience and discomfort we might be causing him.

"The problem is," I explained, "that if we let all the air out of it tonight, we waste a lot of good fishing time pumping the raft back up again in the morning."

"Bamf phoof!" the man replied, apparently not satisfied with my explanation.

"Be careful with that moose head," I warned Clifford. "The horns are messing up the lady's hairdo."

"Sorry, ma'am," Clifford said. "This is the first moose I ever shot, and I like to take it with me wherever I go. Guess I'm just sentimental."

"We'd have left the raft and moose head at the car, but we didn't want them to get stolen," I explained. "You can't tell what kind of people you'll find in one of these hotels."

The man squeezed his head out from behind the raft. "I can't disagree with that," he snapped. From his tone, I judged that he himself had suffered at the hands of some disreputable types in hotels, but as he seemed on the verge of rupturing an important artery, I chose not to pursue the subject with him.

The rest of the evening passed without incident, I'm happy to report. Oh, there was that business with the sheriff and his deputy, but it didn't amount to much.

First of all, Clifford headed back to the car to bring in the rest of our gear. As I've often told him, he should pay more attention to where he is going. Clutching an armful of gear on his return, he glanced over his shoulder as he walked down the hall behind a lady guest. He later said he thought he had heard a noise behind him and expected Retch to be sneaking up to pull some stunt on him with the moose head, because that's the sort of thing Retch thinks is amusing. As far as I know, the lady in the tight evening gown never gave a satisfactory explanation as to why she suddenly stopped and bent over, but I gathered from later testimony that it had something to do with smoothing a wrinkle in her nylons. Now, I have been prodded with the butt end of a

fishing rod on occasion and don't think it anything to raise
a great fuss over. The lady, however, apparently found the
experience new and exhilarating, because she emitted a shrill
yelp and bounded into the air as though from a trampoline.
Clifford, looking back over his shoulder at the time, had no
idea he was even involved in the incident, much less the
culprit. His first impression was that he was being set upon
by a crazy woman intent on flailing him to death with her
purse. It is quite understandable, then, that he should attempt to hold her at bay, fencing style, with a section of
fly rod.

Later that evening, Clifford and I were returning from
reviving ourselves in the hotel bar when another minor incident occurred. We had just stepped out of the elevator
when Clifford suddenly got the punchline of a joke I'd told
him an hour before and burst out in a loud and unexpected
guffaw. The couple ahead of us, dressed to the hilt in evening attire, didn't even look back, but picked up their pace
considerably. Just as they were passing a linen closet, a
moose stuck its head out and said, "Pardon me, but can
you direct me to the nearest restroom?"

"Gee, I thought it was you guys," Retch explained. "I
heard Clifford laugh."

"It was a dumb stunt," I scolded. "That scream almost
deafened me."

"The lady took it pretty well, though," Retch said. "She
probably has a sense of humor, which is more than I can
say for her hubby."

Naturally, both of these incidents were reported to the
hotel manager. The clerk came and told us that we would
have to leave the premises immediately, but we refused on
the grounds that we couldn't possibly take a dying man out
into the rain.

Retch was contemplating whether he needed a shower, having had one the previous week, when the sheriff and his deputy arrived. They turned out to be good fellows, readily accepted our explanations of the two unfortunate incidents, and then joined us in our room to finish off a fifth of Old Thumsucker and exchange a few fishing yarns, both of them now being off duty. The sheriff had a laugh like a bull, and I expected the clerk to come pounding on the door at any instant to hush the lawman up, but not a peep was heard from that strange fellow the rest of the night. An ensuing poker game lasted until three in the morning, at which point the sheriff and his deputy had cleaned us out. Every time the sheriff won a hand, which was on the rare occasions his deputy didn't, he let go with a roar that must have caused the other hotel guests to levitate a foot out of their beds. We tried to get the deputy to wrestle Retch for his share of the winnings against our raft, but the deputy said he didn't even want to touch, let alone wrestle, a man who had a tattoo like Retch's on his chest. The sheriff said he didn't blame the deputy one bit, and furthermore, if Retch didn't get some buttons on his shirt he'd have to arrest him for indecent exposure.

"What is that, anyway?" the sheriff asked, wrinkling up his face.

"Just a little Spanish epigram," I said.

"Huh," the sheriff said. "I coulda swore it was pig."

When we awoke at six, Retch Sweeney seemed like his old self once again, and demonstrated his fitness for us by doing a hundred pushups. "You wanta see me do a hundred with my other arm?" he asked, but Clifford and I were convinced that our friend had recovered from his infirmity, both of us remarking with some amazement upon the healing effects of a night of undisturbed sleep in tranquil surroundings.

The manager and the clerk were at the checkout desk as we prepared to depart the premises. They were unshaven and rumpled and appeared to have put in a miserable night, although neither of them volunteered to inform us about the harrowing experience that had reduced them to this pitiful state. Both of them wore terrible smiles, made all the more awful by the uncontrolled quivering of their lips.

"It's none of our business," I told them, "but if you fellows are in any sort of trouble we might be able to help you out. If somebody's giving you a rough time . . ."

"No! No!" squeaked the manager. "Everything is fine. Just check out and be on your way. Very nice having you gentlemen as guests."

"Well, I'll tell you," I said, "we've a bit of a problem. You see we got in a poker game with the sheriff and his deputy and they won all our money. About all we can do is give you our raft here and this fine moose head to boot. They're worth a few hundred bucks."

"I couldn't think of taking your raft," the manager said, "nor your moose either. We'll just forget the bill. Your visit is on the house, what's left of it."

"That's mighty decent of you," Clifford said. "But we still got a problem. We're gonna be down here fishin' for a couple more days. We got a tent to sleep in, but do you suppose you could loan us a twenty for eatin' money?"

"Gentlemen," said the manager, "we'd be delighted to loan you a twenty for eating money, if it will hasten you on your way."

Well, as I like to say, you can't judge a book by its cover and the same goes for hotels. That manager and his clerk revealed themselves to be real folks after all. And I told them so. I said if any of the three of us was ever in the area on vacation we'd make a point of staying at their hotel. The manager was so taken aback by this sincere expression of appreciation and sentiment that he appeared on the verge of dropping into a dead faint.

As we were walking to our car, a busload of new guests arrived. Retch gave the passengers a friendly wave, causing his buttonless shirt to flare open. It created quite an uproar on the bus, many of the passengers shouting vehemently at the driver. The bus screeched out of the parking lot and headed back down the highway, leaving us standing in a cloud of diesel fumes. While I was scratching my head and trying to guess the reason for such peculiar conduct, I happened to notice a banner strung across the portal of the hotel. It said: CUTIE POOH RESORT WELCOMES THE STATE'S HIGH SCHOOL SPANISH TEACHERS.

A Brief History of Giving (1942-89)

Age eight: I have yet in my life to give anybody a gift. I have not even thought about giving anybody a gift. By some happy stroke of fate, I have been exclusively on the receiving end of gifts. I am happy with this arrangement and see no reason to change it.

Age nine: Mother tells me the time has come when I should start giving Christmas presents to other members of the immediate family. We argue. She wins.

Mother gives me three dollars to buy presents for my sister, grandmother, and herself. The Saturday before Christmas I go to town to shop for gifts. I am tense, confused. Then I find the perfect gift for my sister. Christmas money now reduced to $2.95.

Stress of shopping makes me hungry. Contemplate eating half of sister's gift, but resist temptation. Drop into Nie-

man's Soda Fountain and calm my nerves with banana split.
Christmas funds now reduced to $2.70 but nerves calm.

Return to shopping in decisive mood. Buy grandmother
five skeins of embroidery thread—my first thoughtful gift.
("Oh, how thoughtful!") Buy Mother exquisite little red
glass cup—my first expensive gift. ("Oh, you shouldn't
have!") Relax with hot dog and Coke. Both I and Christmas funds exhausted.

Age ten: My previous Christmas gifts a big hit. So buy
sister another candy bar, grandmother five skeins of embroidery thread, and Mother exquisite little red glass cup.
("Well, it's the thought that counts.") Starting to get the
hang of Christmas shopping.

Age eleven: Acquire girlfriend—first serious relationship
with opposite sex. Become aware of relationship when Betty
Swartz whispers to me that Ruthie likes me. I smile nonchalantly and break out in cold sweat. No girl has ever liked
me before. This is heady stuff. Word spreads fast that Ruthie
and I like each other. I can think of little else.

Ruthie is one of the most beautiful girls in the sixth grade.
I'm the envy of all the guys to whom I've spread the word
that Ruthie likes me. I wonder if I should consummate the
relationship by actually speaking to Ruthie. Decide to wait;
no sense crowding her at this fragile stage.

Hear rumor that Ruthie plans to give me present for
Christmas. Cripes! Lie awake nights worrying about
whether I should give Ruthie a present. What if it's all a
big joke? Maybe Ruthie doesn't intend to give me a present
at all. Maybe she doesn't even like me. Cripes! But what if
Ruthie gives me a present and I don't give her one? Cripes!
I'd better give her a present, but what? I have no idea what
girls like. Ask Mother. She says all girls like nice soap, that
I can't miss with nice soap. I don't know much more about

soap than I do about girls, but buy Ruthie the nicest soap I can find and gift wrap it, with a little pink bow on top.

At recess the last day before Christmas vacation, Ruthie and I exchange presents. I smile nonchalantly, Ruthie giggles. I sense that soon we will actually talk. Ruthie's present to me turns out to be a Big Little Book, a genre I gave up some years before, but it's the thought that counts. By the end of the day, word comes to me that Ruthie has broken off our relationship. She doesn't like me anymore.

I report the failed romance to Mother. "You gave her *what*? Three bars of Lifebuoy!" Mother walks away shaking her head. Just my luck to have my first affair with the one girl in the world who doesn't like soap.

Age twelve: Christmas shopping for the family is no easier; more complicated if anything. Sister's allergy has cleared up, and she is now allowed to eat candy. Mother informs me she herself has an adequate, perhaps even excessive, supply of exquisite little red glass cups. On the plus side, grandmother says she may soon take up embroidery as a hobby.

Age thirty: Have gradually begun to master the two basic types of gifts: the thoughtful and the expensive, and their respective difficulties. Realize that nothing is gained by combining the two. Each stands on its own merits. To pour both thought and expense into a single gift is to waste either thinking or money. You don't have to expend any thought on a diamond bracelet for a wife or girlfriend, or on a sports car for your kid. They will be happy with an expensive gift even if it is totally thoughtless. (I suppose there are families of sufficient wealth where a wife might say, "A sable stole! How thoughtful of you, Fred!" or the kid might say, "Gee, Dad, how thoughtful—a Ferrari.")

The expense of the expensive gift, of course, must be

apparent. It is unwise, I learn, to pay big bucks for an antique pine chest that may turn out to be identical to one the recipient's grandparents are currently using for a cat box. If I pay four hundred dollars for a gift, it better shout out "Four hundred dollars!" loud and clear. Otherwise, I might as well go with a thoughtful gift.

Being of modest means in this period of my life, I am limited to giving thoughtful (cheap) gifts. The thoughtful gift, alas, involves the tedium of actually thinking about the recipient at some length, in order to match the gift to his or her life-style, hobby, occupation, or emotional state of the moment. As I now know, one must be particularly wary of thoughtful gifts that may imply unintended statements about the recipient's character or, worse yet, make rude remarks about his or her habits of personal hygiene. That is why gifts of soap, or handkerchiefs for that matter, should be avoided. ("A box of handkerchiefs? Is he trying to tell me . . . ?") Indeed, gifts that make statements of any kind are fraught with risk. My policy now is to select only those gifts that know how to keep their mouths shut.

Age forty: Begin teaching the art of giving. Wife buys expensive wood bowl for friend, Frieda, who's done her a special favor. Bowl is hand-carved out of wood so rare only five other pieces exist in the world, four under lock and key in the Vatican. Carving personally signed by dead artist, Leonardo da Vinci Perkins, whose name is spoken in hushed reverence by aficionados of wood-bowl carving.

Wife begins wrapping gift. Using Socratic method, I attempt to instruct her on the art of expensive giving.

"Am I correct in assuming Frieda knows her woods pretty well?" I ask gently.

"Frieda couldn't tell a two-by-four from a sheet of plywood."

"I see. Wouldn't she have perhaps developed an interest in rare woods while studying the works of Leonardo da Vinci Perkins?"

"Frieda? She's never even heard of Perkins."

"Hmmmm. Do you think it might be a good idea to insert the receipt for the bowl somewhere in the wrapping as though it had slipped in there by accident?"

"That's so crude and disgusting only you would think of it!"

"True. But do you perhaps see any resemblance between this work of art and the bowl our daughter Erin turned out in high school shop class when she was a sophomore? Is it at all possible that Frieda might think this a thoughtful gift related to her gardening, drill a drain hole in the bottom, and plant petunias in it?"

"Well, don't just stand there yacking. Go get the receipt out of my purse while I undo an edge of the wrapping."

Age fifty-five: There are now eighty-seven different occasions and several hundred people for whom I must buy gifts throughout the course of each year. If I go on a trip with my wife, I am for some unknown reason expected to buy gifts for all the relatives, friends, and casual acquaintances who didn't get to go on the trip with us. That is what my wife tells me. Our neighbors move to the next town to buy a new house. We get them a going-away present and then a housewarming present. We buy presents for people who are going to get married and again when they get married, for people who are going to have a baby and again when they have the baby. It seems endless. Half my waking hours would be spent shopping for gifts if I hadn't reduced the process to a science: I let my wife buy all the presents. Occasionally, though, I go gift shopping with her to offer my services as a consultant.

"How do you think your sister would like this blouse?"
she asks. "Is it her? Or do you think it's a bit too frilly?
Perhaps if we found something in a pink—"

"It's her," I advise, rearranging my hairline in a mirror.
"Buy it."

Gift shopping has become incredibly easy in recent years,
even when I must go alone in search of a present for my
wife. Fortunately, she has a fondness for exquisite little red
glass cups. As she likes to say, it's the thought that counts.

Pouring My Own

Some years ago, I bought a little house in the country, because my wife said it was "perfect." An hour after closing the deal, Bun said there was only one small problem with the house.

"I thought it was perfect," I said.

"It is," she replied. "But I don't like the little dirt path that leads to the back door."

"I like it," I said. "It says 'country' to me."

"It says 'dirt' to me. Put in a concrete walk."

I called a contractor who specialized in concrete work. The man turned out to be an amateur comic. He would not be serious. The price he gave me for a thirty-foot walk obviously was intended to get a laugh. I refused him even a chuckle in response, hoping to discourage any further attempts at humor. "Seriously, though, how much would you charge?" I asked. He quoted the same absurd price. The man would not let go of what he obviously thought a wonderful gag. So I gave up on him.

"I'll pour the walk myself," I told Bun. "It can't be that difficult. I'll slap together a form out of some two-by-fours, dump in some premix concrete, smooth it all up, and—presto!—a concrete walk!"

"And—presto!—a disaster!" she snapped. "Pay the man what he asks!"

"No, I will not," I said. "After all, it isn't as though I haven't had experience pouring concrete. I poured the patio at our last house and it didn't turn out too badly."

"Yeah, as a poor imitation of a Henry Moore reclining sculpture!"

"So, you can't have everything. Besides, I ran into some unforeseen problems."

There are many unforeseen problems working with concrete. The wonderful thing about it is that you know whatever you make may last a thousand years. That, of course, can also be one of its major disadvantages. The recipe for concrete consists of mixing unknown quantities of water with one part cement, three parts sand, five parts gravel, and ten parts cold sweat. The cold sweat results from the fact that wet concrete contains its own ticking version of a time bomb. When the clock runs out, the concrete hardens into permanence, without regard for your desires or feelings. It has no mercy. It doesn't say, "Oh, I see, you wanted a nice flat smooth concrete floor, and I'm still in the shape of surf. I'll just hold off hardening for another hour." No, concrete doesn't say that. If the clock runs out while the concrete is in the shape of surf, you get surf—surf that will last a thousand years!

Back when I was a teenager, a carpenter hired me to help

him pour a concrete floor in a dairy barn. The premix trucks brought too much concrete too soon too fast, which is their standard practice. Here I must say a word about the drivers of concrete trucks. Before being hired, they are required to sit through all the Marx Brothers movies. If they crack so much as a smile at the wild antics on the screen, they are immediately disqualified for employment. The reason for this is that the owners of concrete companies believe it is bad for business to have their drivers writhing on the ground in paroxysms of mirth induced by the frenzied antics of the recipients of too much concrete too soon too fast.

Because they had other orders to fill, the drivers dumped the concrete in great gray oozing heaps at one end of the dairy barn. The carpenter released a strangled cry of horror, grabbed a shovel and wheelbarrow, and turned into a streaking blur of motion, depositing dabs of concrete here and there about the form but without reducing the gray heaps noticeably. Despite their training, a couple of the drivers broke into smiles, and one had to bite his lip to keep from laughing outright. Knowing nothing about the nature of concrete, I stood gawking at the carpenter's amazing performance, unsure of whether I was expected to applaud. Suddenly the blur halted a few inches from my face, and a crazed wild creature emerged, sweat streaming down over its bulging red eyes and dribbling off its quivering jowls. It barked sharply at me. Supposing that my life was in danger, I too grabbed a shovel and wheelbarrow and began moving concrete, although not with the same enthusiasm as the creature. By midnight, the floor was done. It was not unattractive. The gray waves undulated rhythmically from one end of the barn to the other, here and there crashing against a wall or storage bin, and at other places settling into hard rippling pools, havens of calm on the edge of a receding storm. The farmer who owned the barn, however, was a practical man, and not much given to aesthetic appreciation. He expressed the opinion, rather sullenly I thought, that his cows would churn their own butter just walking to their stanchions. Hoping to introduce a bit of levity into a tense situation, I told him he might like the floor better if he painted it blue, possibly with blotches of white scattered about to suggest foam. He responded only by glaring at me and grinding his teeth. I judged from his expression that he didn't think highly of our work, although that is only conjecture. Personally, I thought the floor turned out pretty well, particularly considering that it was the work of an inexperienced teenage boy and a crazed wild creature.

One of the reasons I'd run into unforeseen problems pouring the patio was that I'd read this how-to pamphlet on pouring concrete. The author, who's apparently still on the loose (stop him before he writes again!), made pouring concrete sound about as complicated as making mud pies. It is, in fact, serious work. It takes careful preparation and planning, the neglect of which had caused most of my troubles with the patio. I would not make the same mistake pouring the walk. Every single little step and calculation would be worked out to the nth degree.

"Here's the plan," I told Bun. "I'll eliminate the middle man. I'll go down to the tool-rental company and rent a special trailer for hauling premix concrete. The company will place just enough concrete in the trailer for my walk, for which I have worked out the exact specifications. I tow the trailer home, run my wheelbarrow up under the spout, open the gate, the concrete flows smoothly into my wheelbarrow, and I then wheel the wheelbarrow over to my forms

and dump it. When the forms are full, I level off the concrete and smooth it up. Presto! A concrete walk! Simple as
making mud pies.''

"Where have I heard that before?'' she asked.

I nipped off to the tool rental place and soon returned with a
trailer full of concrete. A crowd of spectators had gathered to
watch the pouring of the walk, mostly neighborhood children
but also a few mothers, who had tagged a long "just for the
laughs,'' as one of them joshingly put it. Why my efforts at
serious work should be regarded as a source of comedy in the
neighborhood, I don't know. Not wishing to disappoint the
entertainment-starved wretches, however, I grabbed my wheelbarrow with a theatrical flourish and attempted to run it up
under the trailer's spout. But the spout was six inches too low
for my wheelbarrow! Already I could hear the tick-tick-tick of
the concrete hardening inside the trailer. Refusing to panic, I
ripped a few boards off the side of my garage and built a six-
inch high ramp to back the trailer onto. The trailer crushed the
ramp like a house of toothpicks, provoking the spectators to
laughter and applause.

"Do it again!'' one little bugger chirped. "Do it again!''

Panic now seeming the proper response to the situation,
I snatched up a shovel and dug a slanted trench beneath the
spout, spewing dirt over the spectators and half the yard.
Mothers clamped hands over the ears of children. "What's
he saying, Momma?'' a nipper cried. "What kind of concrete did he say it was?''

With suspense building, primarily in me, I grabbed the
wheelbarrow, ran it down the trench, and opened the gate
to the spout. Not a drop of concrete flowed forth.

The audience dispersed. That they fled for their lives is part
of the myth of the neighborhood, with no more basis in fact

than the imaginative reports that I turned into a crazed wild creature. My own recollection is that I greeted the predicament with icy calm. In fact, I clearly recall staring at the sign on the trailer that warned of a twenty-five dollar fee if the trailer was returned "unclean." I wondered if a solid cubic yard of concrete inside the trailer qualified as unclean.

Fortunately, only the outer layer of concrete had solidified to the point where it refused to flow. By gouging at this outer crust with my shovel (I would by no means describe this effort as "frenzied," a word often misused by Bun), I was able to release a sluggish stream of concrete into my wheelbarrow. I realized, of course, that the ticking time bomb of the concrete was ticking its last ticks. Haste was called for. Haste came.

And presto!—a concrete walk! The casual observer of the walk, however, might have assumed it was something else, possibly a free-form imaginative work, with textures varying from near smooth to rough to lumpy. Here and there twigs protruded from the concrete, which also entombed partially or wholly one child's sneaker, one work glove, a Timex with a broken strap, countless leaves, several thousand insects (small squiggles in the concrete attested to their last desperate struggles), and possibly a cat, whose mysterious disappearance coincided with the pouring of the walk. Once again, a courageous do-it-yourselfer had gone forth to slay the dragon of concrete and returned burnt to a crisp.

But Bun said she thought the walk would work just fine for as long as it lasted.

"Yeah," I said. "It's really not too bad. Heck, that walk could last a thousand years!"

"Three days," Bun said. "That's the soonest the demolition men can come."

Teenagers From Hell

It is a terrible thing to be a teenager, without resources of your own. The world is your oyster, but you can't pry it out of its shell. All those wonderful Firsts of life you hunger to experience gleam like gold scarcely a stone's throw away, but between you and those treasures stand fire-breathing creatures known as parents. "NO!" the creatures roar. "NO! NO! NO!"

"NO!" roared Mr. Sweeney. "NO! NO!"

His son, Retch, and I stepped back away from him to prevent our eyebrows getting singed. Upon his arriving home tired and sweaty from work, some vague activity Mr. Sweeney engaged in because "money don't grow on trees," Retch and I had presented him with a wonderful plan. We would take his fishing car and drive it up to his little lake cabin, where we would take the cedar-strip boat he had built himself and his new five-horse outboard motor, and go fishing with his good fishing tackle, just the two of us, alone for the first time, without Mr. Sweeney hovering over us and shouting out "NO! NO!" at regular intervals.

"C'mon, Popper, just this once," Retch pleaded. "We won't hurt nothin'."

"Absolutely not!" shouted Mr. Sweeney. "There's no way I'm going to let you two loons destroy my car, my cabin, my boat and my new motor, and my good fishing tackle. I'll tell you what," he said, turning down the volume a few notches. "You wait until next weekend, and I'll take the two of you up there fishing. How does that sound?"

"But that's no fun, Popper. We want to do it by ourselves. How are we ever going to learn if we don't do stuff by ourselves?"

Mr. Sweeney turned the volume back up, his response bringing Mrs. Sweeney bounding out to the front porch.

"Herbert! Hush!" she ordered. "What will the neighbors think! Furthermore, I won't stand for you using those words around these impressionable young boys!"

Retch and I tried to look as impressionable as possible, while Mr. Sweeney rolled his eyes beseechingly toward heaven and emitted a shuddering sigh. "Sorry," he said. "But those were the only words that came near to fitting the scheme the loons have cooked up. Know what they have the audacity to ask? They want to . . ."

"Yes, I know, go up to your cabin for a little fishing. I think it's a perfectly reasonable request. Wouldn't you rather have them up at the cabin doing some wholesome fishing instead of hanging out down at the pool hall with a bunch of wild girls?"

"No, I would not! I hung out down at the pool hall when I was a kid, and look at me. I ain't turned out so bad. Why, heck, speaking of wild girls, look at . . ."

"Herbert! Hush!"

"I just don't see why I should have to loan them my fishing car, my cabin, my boat, and my motor," Mr. Sweeney said to his wife. "If you're so dad-blamed set on them enjoying themselves, why don't you loan them your . . . uh . . . your . . . uh . . . your washing machine or your . . . uh . . . your vacuum cleaner?"

Mrs. Sweeney smiled. "Anytime, Herbert, anytime. Now quit being a stingy old grouch and help the boys get your fishing car loaded."

Mr. Sweeney wasn't much help getting his gear loaded into his fishing car. Mostly, he hovered about whispering vague threats to Retch and me. "You loons put one scratch on this car and, well, you just wait and see. Anything happens to my boat and motor . . . ! You leave that cabin a mess and . . . !" I guess Mr. Sweeney didn't want to tell us the specific horrible consequences because of our being so impressionable.

At last the car was packed, and we were ready to go. Mrs. Sweeney came out to see us off. She stood there with her arm around her husband, who was clenching and unclenching his fists as though each was around a tiny neck. They made a cute couple, Mr. and Mrs. Sweeney. Old but cute. Seeing the two of them standing there together must have touched a soft spot in Retch.

"So long, Mommer," he said. "And we really appreciate your letting us use all your stuff, Popper. You're one nice father. Me and you don't always get along too good, I know, but there's something I need to tell you."

Mrs. Sweeney smiled up at her husband, a tiny tear trembling in the corner of her eye.

"Yeah? What?" Mr. Sweeney said, gruffly, sounding slightly embarrassed.

"Only this, Popper. The fishing car's almost out of gas. How about giving us a few bucks for gas money?"

Driving up to the fishing cabin, I said to Retch, "I noticed your father used those words again. Where did he learn words like that, anyway?"

"Marine Corps," Retch said. "They teach those words in boot camp. Use them to scare the enemy."

"They scared me," I said.

"Me too," Retch said. "But they're supposed to. We're the enemy."

Retch and I arrived at the lake cabin just before dark and went inside and started a fire. Luckily, we were able to smother it before it did much damage.

"I don't know why Popper doesn't buy a new gas lantern," Retch said, rubbing off his eyebrows.

"Well, he'll have to now," I said. "The flames shot darn near to the ceiling. Good thing you had wits enough to throw your dad's fishing vest on top of it before you booted it out the door. Might have touched off a forest fire otherwise."

"You didn't do too bad yourself, tossing that bucket of water on the burning floorboards. The whole cabin could have gone up like a torch!"

The next morning we dragged the little cedar-strip boat down to the lake and launched it. It was one of the prettiest boats I'd ever seen, about what you'd expect of something that had been lovingly crafted with hand tools over a period of five years or so. It rowed like a dream. But the five-horse motor sent it skimming up the lake like a shaft of golden light playing on the waves. The fishing was wonderful, too. By evening we had two heavy stringers of perch and crappy. Night was oozing in around us by the time we started back down the lake. Retch was rowing.

"Bail a little faster," he said. "We're taking on too much water."

"I'm bailing as fast as I can," I said. "You wouldn't think a little hole like that would let in so much water."

"Darn snag," Retch said. "Not only does it get the boat, it nails the motor, too. I've been up here a dozen times with Popper, and he's never once mentioned that snag. You would think a person's father would mention an obstacle like that. No, all he does is shout. 'Not so fast, not so fast! You'll run into something!' I tell you it makes me feel bad to see that kind of negligence in a person's own parent. Bail faster!"

"Row faster!"

We finally made it back to the cabin, with a good three or four inches of the boat showing above water. We tied up at the dock, threw what was left of Mr. Sweeney's gear in the car, and headed home. Now, I certainly didn't recall seeing that big rock in the road on our way to the cabin. Retch said he was certain that it hadn't been there. The wrecker man said it had probably fallen down off the mountain after we had gone past on our way to the cabin. "Because," he said, "any fool would have noticed a rock that size."

The rock had gone right under the car, ripping off assorted parts, some of which were apparently fairly important, because the car refused to run.

"Can you fix it?" I asked the wrecker man.

"Fix it?" he said. "Only God could fix that car, and His

bill would be almost as much as mine. You say a Mr. Herbert Sweeney will be happy to pay for my services, right? You boys just stand where I can see you until this Mr. Sweeney arrives, okay?''

"Okay," Retch said. "But unless you have a strong stomach, I think it would be better if he picked us up down the road a ways.''

An hour after a collect phone call to the Sweeney residence, Mr. Sweeney's other car came roaring into the gas station. Mr. Sweeney got out and stood there for a moment staring at us. I wished he had been a little more specific about the consequences of our destroying his belongings. Then he rushed at us.

"You're both still alive!" he cried. "No missing limbs, no broken bones?''

"Naw, Popper, we're okay," Retch said, cringing. "But we destroyed your fishing car.''

"That piece of junk! Good riddance!''

"And we hit a snag and broke a hole in your boat and knocked out your new motor. The boat's mostly sunk but tied up at the dock.''

"You managed to get it back to the dock? That's wonderful! I thought I'd never see it or the motor again!''

"And we had a fire in the cabin, but we got it put out before it did much damage.''

"You mean you didn't burn the cabin to the ground? I can't believe it? This is fantastic! And you two loons are still alive to tell about it! I never thought it could happen! Maybe you guys are actually ready to go out on your own, without me tagging along all the time. By gosh, I can hardly believe you made it back alive. What a relief!''

Driving back home with his father, Retch and I slowly

recovered from the shocks of the day. Indeed, the good cheer of Mr. Sweeney proved infectious, and soon Retch and I were giving him a hilarious account of our adventure, to which Mr. Sweeney responded with great mirth.

"And then I kicked the lantern right out the door," Retch said, "and busted it all to smithereens. Har har har!"

"Kicked it out the door and busted it all to smithereens!" shouted Mr. Sweeney. "Har har har!"

"But wait, there's more," Retch said, wiping tears from his eyes. "We put out the fire with your old fishing vest! Burnt a big hole in it! Heee heeee!"

"Burnt a hole in my old fishing vest?" Mr. Sweeney said, not laughing. "Burnt a hole in my fishing vest! Don't press your luck, Retch, don't press your luck!"

As Retch said later, that was the problem with parents. All they cared about were their dumb old possessions.

Secret Places

All my life I have had secret places. I like secret places. They make me feel smug and superior, two of the really great feelings.

"I've got this secret place," you tell a friend. Right away he wants to know where it is. "I can't tell you," you say, smugly, superiorly. "It's a secret."

I also hate secret places—other people's. Ross Russell has a secret hunting place I've been trying to pry out of him for years.

"C'mon, Ross, you can tell me," I say. "I won't ever sneak up there to hunt without you. We've been friends for forty years. What are friends for, if not to tell their secret hunting places? Just tell me, okay?"

"Can't. It's a secret."

"Tell me your secret hunting place if you want to live!"

I have about three dozen secret places scattered around

the country. Some are nothing more than small, gravelly beaches; others are entire mountain valleys and even mountain ranges. Often, I come across other people in my secret places. They, of course, have just as much right to be there as I do. It's very irritating.

I suppose it's all right to share your secret places with strangers, as long as you don't have to share the secret.

When I was a boy, I loved secret places even more than I do now. Within a three-mile radius of our farm, I had staked out hundreds of secret places—fishing holes, hunting spots, caves, swamps, lookout trees, old cabins, and even several culverts under the highway. Some of my secret spots were shared with particular friends.

"This will be our secret spot," I would say to my friend. "Nobody else will know about it."

"Okay," he would say. Then we would take a spit oath. If I had taken a blood oath for every one of my secret spots I shared with someone, I would have been a quart low most of the time. Besides, spit oaths are much less painful than blood oaths. Occasionally, I would fall off a cow or a pig or something and end up with a bloody nose. That was the only time I cared about taking a blood oath.

"Let's say this is our secret spot and take a blood oath on it," I'd tell Crazy Eddie Muldoon as I tried to dam the flow of blood from a nostril.

"In the middle of a cow pasture?" he'd say. "This isn't a good secret place."

"It's good enough," I'd reply. "I want to take a blood oath on it. So cut your finger."

"I don't want to cut my finger, not for a blood oath on a secret place in the middle of a lousy cow pasture. Why don't we both just use your blood?"

"Okay." Eddie had the right instincts.

Secret spots seldom had any special use other than to be secret. Fishing holes made good secret spots and were useful, but mostly what we did in secret spots was to sit around in them feeling smug and superior. It was quite evident to us that half the population of the world was simply dying to know the location of our secret spot, and that was sufficient for us.

Crazy Eddie and I did find one secret spot that we put to excellent use. One day we crawled up to the naked joists in the Muldoon garage. There were a few boards scattered around on the joists to walk on, so we walked on them, holding our arms out like tightrope walkers to maintain our balance and keep from smashing our skulls on the concrete floor below. We came to a sheet of plywood laid over the joists like an island in the air and stopped there to rest. There were some boxes stacked on the sheet of plywood and we sat down on them.

"Hey, you know what, Eddie," I said. "This would make a great secret place for us."

"Yeah," he said. "Good idea. We can come up here and . . . and . . . well, we can come up here."

"Sure," I said. "This would be perfect for that. Hey, what's in the boxes?"

Eddie lifted a lid. "Just some empty canning jars."

"Maybe we can think of something to do with them."

Eddie smiled. "I got an idea. We could fill them."

"Fill them with what?"

Eddie explained what we could fill them with.

"Hey, that's good," I said. "It will be kind of like scientific research. We can see how long it takes us to fill all these jars." Eddie and I started our research immediately, and managed to fill one of the jars about one-third full, which wasn't bad, considering we were acting on short notice. We screwed the lid back on the jar and set it neatly back in its box. Scientific research was fun.

The project was started in late spring. We worked on it well into the hot days of summer. Our dedication was enormous. A group of us kids would be fishing off the Sand Creek bridge, and Eddie would say, "Oh oh, I've got to go to the bathroom." Then he would leap on his bicycle and ride madly off toward the secret place in his garage, where I knew he would climb the ladder, balance his way across the boards on the ceiling joists to the sheet of plywood, and make a contribution to the scientific project.

The other kids would stare after Eddie as he pedaled frantically off up Sand Creek Hill. "How come Eddie rides his bike all the way home to go to the bathroom?" someone would ask me, this not being the standard practice of the group.

"Can't tell you," I'd say. "Eddie and I are conducting a secret scientific experiment in our secret place."

"C'mon, tell us!"

"Nope. Can't. It's a secret." I'd feel smug and superior all over.

One sizzling hot July day, I asked Eddie what the count was now.

"Thirty-nine full and a good start on the fortieth. But we're almost out of jars."

"Maybe you could ask your mom for some more empty jars," I suggested.

"Maybe."

We headed for Eddie's house to ask his mom for some more empty jars. As we were passing the open door of the Muldoon garage, we noticed Mr. Muldoon's legs disappearing up a ladder in the direction of our secret place. Pretty soon we could hear him tramping across the narrow board walkway on the ceiling joists.

"What are you doing up there, Pa?" Eddie called out nervously. Obviously, Mr. Muldoon had no idea he was violating a secret place.

"Oh, I stored a couple of planks up here. Stay where you are. I may need some help getting them down." He stepped onto the plywood sheet that formed the floor to our secret place. "Now what's this. Well, I'll be dang. Your ma's got some kind of canned goods stored up here. Why would she put it up here instead of in the cellar? Looks like some kind of juice. I don't know what's got into that woman. This stuff's probably spoiled, simmering up here in this heat. I better open a jar and see what it is."

Eddie and I looked at each other. He could tell I was winding up my mainspring that would shoot me off home. "Pa," he said, "I don't think you should—"

We heard the tinny *plink* of a lid popping off a canning jar, followed by a strangled, choking shout from Mr. Muldoon. We could hear him staggering about, then crashing into the crate of jars. The jars tumbled down onto the concrete floor in a series of magnificent golden explosions. Powerful toxic fumes filled the garage, bringing tears to our eyes. *"Aaaack!"* cried Mr. Muldoon, who apparently thought he, too, was being destroyed. We watched in horror as he leaped about in a series of pirouettes on the naked joists above, until at last he dropped into a space between them, luckily catching himself by the armpits. He then hung by his hands and dropped to the floor, apparently spraining both ankles, or so I judged from the manner in which he came hobbling out of the clouds of fumes, choking and gasping.

"Pa! Pa!" shouted Eddie. "You destroyed our experiment! A whole summer's work!"

A rare moment of insight into the peculiar workings of Mr. Muldoon's mind told me that the destruction of our summer's work was the least of our concerns. "Got to go home," I said to Eddie.

"Oh, okay," he said. "See you later."

As I released my mainspring and shot by Mr. Muldoon, who was hunched over choking and coughing and wiping his streaming nose and eyes, I very much doubted whether Eddie had a later.

One of the best things you can do with a secret place is share it with a special friend. Sometimes, though, you don't even like the person you choose to share a secret place with. It is one of those strange psychological aberrations beyond human comprehension.

My father died when I was six. Five years later, my mother remarried. I did not much care for my new step-father at first. The only good thing about Hank was that he liked to fish, even though he wasn't very good at it. From time to time, he would take me fishing and try to make amends for rudely invading my domain, but I wasn't having any of it. We almost never caught any fish anyway.

Hank was so poor at fishing he was ecstatic whenever he caught so much as a little seven-inch trout, and he would even tell the neighbors about this fish he had caught. It was embarrassing. I hated to go places with him, it was so embarrassing to hear him tell his fish stories. He didn't even know how to lie properly: he would go into all the details about how he had baited his hook and dropped it into the current just so and let it drift down behind a sunken stump, and then describe the thrilling strike of the fish.

"Gosh, how big was that fish, Hank?" the neighbor would ask.

Lie, Hank! I'd plead silently. *Lie!*

"Oh, a good seven inches," Hank would say truthfully.

"Umm," the neighbor would politely respond.

Stream fishing opened the first week of June. Huge cutthroat trout continued their spawning run up Sand Creek for exactly a week after the opening. One day the cutthroats would be there, and the next they would be gone. Hank knew nothing about the run of big trout. When opening day arrived, he was prepared to go out after another seven-incher. It was bad enough that I had to put up with a new stepfather. I simply couldn't stand the further embarrassment of listening to him tell his small-fish stories, particularly to fishermen who would have spent the day hauling out huge cutthroat.

Before first light on opening day, Hank and I headed down to Sand Creek. Practically the entire town had emptied out and now lined the banks of the creek to have a go at the cutthroat. Hank, of course, thought everybody was after his seven-incher.

"Cripes," he said. "I think I'll go back home. We'd have to stand in line to get a chance to cast into the crick." Because Hank had never seen anybody else fish Sand Creek, he probably had come to think of it as his own secret place. He seemed depressed. Here he'd had his heart set on catching his seven-incher on opening day and now it was ruined for him.

"Good idea, Hank," I said. "You better go home."

He turned and started to walk back to the house.

At that moment I was overcome by one of those weaknesses of character I despise so much in myself. "Wait," I said. "Wait, Hank. I'll take you to my secret place."

"Secret place?" he said. "What secret place?"

There was a large bend in Sand Creek that no one ever fished because the brush was so high and thick that it was assumed to be impassable. It was further assumed that if a person managed to fight his way through the brush, there would be no place to stand to fish the creek. But a couple of days before opening, I had found that I could crawl through the brush on my hands and knees. And on the other side of the brush, I discovered a tiny gravel beach right upstream from a magnificent fishing hole! It was one of the finest secret places I've ever come across.

Half an hour later, Hank and I were crawling through the brush on our hands and knees. I let Hank go first to break trail. With typical clumsiness, he let a branch snap back and hit me in the nose. I could feel the trickle of blood begin to flow. The man was hopeless.

His first five casts, Hank caught five cutthroat all upward of two pounds, one approaching five. He was practically shedding his skin from the pure joy of it. "I can't believe it!" he cried. "This is wonderful! I never realized fish this big even existed!" His eyes were disgustingly moist.

Still dabbing at my bloody nose, I had not yet got a line in the water. Hank hadn't even waited for me to get ready, he was such a fish hog.

"You know what, Pat," he shouted at me. "From now on, this will be our secret place! Just yours and mine!"

"Oh yeah?" I said. "In that case, cut your finger."

"How come?"

" 'Cause we have to take a blood oath on a secret place. Don't you know that?"

Hank stared at me, as his shaking hands unhooked a twenty-inch cutthroat. "Maybe we could both just use your blood," he said. "How does that sound?"

It sounded all right to me. I figured Hank might not turn out too badly after all, with the proper amount of training. He seemed to have the right instincts.

Puttering

When I strolled into the kitchen the other day for a coffee refill my wife, Bun, was on the phone, reaching out and touching her friend Melba.

"Well, I'd better go now," she said. "Himself just walked in. What? Oh, he's been out puttering in his old workshop."

Puttering? *Puttering!*

I certainly was not *puttering* in my workshop. Crafting an exquisite coffee table is not *puttering!* It's fine woodworking. Nothing annoys me more than Bun's misuse of the word "puttering" in reference to my highly skilled use of tools in the creation of elegant furniture pieces. Actually, come to think of it, there are several things about Bun that annoy me more, but her misuse of "puttering" is right up near the top of the list.

Do all wives harbor this amused view of their husband's activities? Does the surgeon's wife say: "Oh, Fred's puttering around in the operating room. Some brain thing."

Did Michelangelo's wife say: "Oh, Mike's puttering around over at the Sistine Chapel."

Did Thomas Jefferson's wife say: "Oh, Tom's down in the living room puttering with some old declaration of independence."

I think not.

I notice that when I'm putting up a shelf in the pantry, Bun doesn't refer to that as puttering. No, that's significant work, putting up a plain old board shelf as any ten-year-old could.

"Maybe I should round off the edges with my new router," I say.

"The plain board's just fine," she says. "An exquisitely crafted shelf would be nice, but I need it now, not next year. You're just looking for an excuse to use that router of yours."

"Very funny," I respond. That's another annoying thing about Bun. She has no appreciation of fine tools, no understanding of the importance of having just the right tool for the particular job. To her, a perfectly balanced hammer is nothing more than a pounder; a pair of first-rate lockgrip pliers, a squeezer. I once heard her say, "Woodworking is merely an excuse for buying tools." Ha! Can you believe it?

My dictionary defines "putter" as "to occupy oneself aimlessly, *to putter around the kitchen.*" The italics, by the way, aren't mine, but those of some lexicographer puttering about with the language. Okay, I'll accept the fact that I occupy myself aimlessly in the kitchen, such as vainly searching through the refrigerator for something that isn't good for me. Occasionally, I'll even think about taking up gourmet cooking for a hobby, and free Bun from the monotonous chore of endless meal preparation.

"I'm fixing dinner tonight," I tell her. "You go take it easy."

"Great!" she says.

"Where are the anchovies?" I ask. "Don't we have any anchovies?"

"No, we don't have anchovies. Never had, never will."

"I guess I'll have to use sardines with the scrambled eggs, then. Where are the taco shells?"

The phone rings. Bun answers it. "Hi, Dave . . . Yeah, he's here . . . Just puttering about the kitchen."

I can accept that. I readily admit that my activities in the kitchen are rather aimless, mostly because I don't know where anything is, and we don't have it anyway. It's not as though I were building an exquisite coffee table or something else of lasting value.

I putter in my workshop, too. Sometimes my concentration's not quite up to working with power tools that can gobble your fingers like corn chips. On those occasions, I'll start sorting screws and putting each size and type into its own container. Baby-food jars are perfect for this.

"Do we have any empty baby-food jars?" I ask Bun.

"Afraid not," she says. "I tossed out the last one—twenty years ago."

Just my luck. While we still had baby-food jars, I couldn't afford screws. Now that I can afford screws, no baby-food jars. How can I sort screws properly if I don't have baby-food jars? I wander aimlessly about looking for other containers.

That's an example of puttering in the workshop.

I decided to straighten Bun out on the proper use of the word "puttering."

"Let's have a little chat," I said. "Grab a cup of coffee and bring it over to the coffee table."

"Okay," she said. "Which one?"

"The one with the checkerboard inlay," I said. "I still have a little touching-up work to do on those other two. Watch the leg! This one's still a little tippy."

"You seem to have a problem coping with legs."

"Yeah. But I can't trim any more off these legs to even them up. The coffee table's only six inches high as it is. At least it's better than setting your coffee cup on the floor."

"On the advice of counsel, I must refuse to comment on that. But the inlay is nice."

"Thanks. Incidentally, you'll be happy to know I just noticed this ad for a leg-leveling device in *Fine Woodworking*. That should solve the problem, and it's such a clever little tool, too."

"That's wonderful. I'm so happy you shared it with me."

"I thought you'd like it. Now, about your use of the word 'puttering' . . ."

Search and—Uh—Rescue

Looking through an old family scrapbook the other day, I came across a yellowed piece of newsprint from my hometown newspaper. It's a photograph of my loutish cousin Buck and a gnomish little man wearing a surplus army coat and a stocking cap. They are standing by a snowbank in front of the *North Idaho Weekly Gazette* building, which is festooned with Christmas decorations. Buck wears his Modest Hero expression, while the man beside him, Henry P. Grogan, the crafty proprietor of Grogan's War Surplus, glowers at the camera.

The headline on the accompanying story reads LOCAL HERO SAVES CITY BUSINESSMAN.

Well.

As an unheralded participant in what I came to think of as "Buck's Big Bungle," I later managed to piece together what I believe to be the germinal misunderstanding. Grogan's wife, Vera, had been explaining to her friend, Mrs. Thompson, how depressed Grogan was that his son, Junior P. Grogan, had gone off and joined the army. Junior, she said, had always accompanied Grogan out to Big Sandy Mountain to cut the family Christmas tree. Indeed, she said, Grogan was at that very minute up on Big Sandy, morosely looking for a Christmas tree all by himself. Then Mrs. Grogan added, "The poor man's lost," meaning, of course, that Grogan was emotionally lost without his son to keep him company. All this might seem quite sad, unless you happened to have known Junior Grogan, whose induction into the army was cause for rejoicing among most of the town's citizenry, Henry P. himself being no exception. If there had been a parade to celebrate the occasion, Grogan would have led it.

Exactly what Mrs. Grogan told Mrs. Thompson remains a matter of speculation. The important thing is that Mrs. Thompson's twelve-year-old son, Willy, heard only parts of the conversation, the parts about Grogan being up on Big Sandy Mountain and being lost. Willy then wandered outside and down the block, where I was helping Buck work on his car in front of Aunt Sophie's house. A major blizzard gusted snow around us as we worked.

"Guess what?" Willy said. He was dressed in about fifty pounds of clothes. I thought mildly about rolling him down the street like a bowling ball.

"Beat it, kid," Buck said, blowing on his hands.

"You know Henry P. Grogan?"

"I said, beat it."

"Well, ol' Grogan's lost up on Big Sandy Mountain."

"Tough," Buck said, tinkering with the engine. "Now,

try it," he said to me. The car gurgled and choked and then exploded into a violent but sustained racket.

"Hey hey hey!" Buck said. "Do I or do I not have the old mechanical knack!"

"Didn't you hear what Willy said?" I asked him. "About Grogan being lost up on Big Sandy?"

"Yeah, so what?" Buck slammed down the hood and ordered me out of the driver's seat. He was about twenty then, and I, sixteen, a circumstance that gave him the privilege of bossing me around, that and the fact that he owned a car for hunting and fishing.

"So maybe we should go up there and look for Grogan," I suggested.

"You must be nuts," Buck said. "If that thieving old buzzard was dumb enough to get himself lost, he can be dumb enough to get himself found. Besides, I have important business to take care of, like getting a date with the new waitress down at the truck stop."

Willy hopped on the running board. "You could be a hero, Buck. You could save Mr. Grogan and then you could go off without giving anybody your name, and everybody would wonder who the mysterious hero had been. It'd be neat!"

Buck and I both stared at Willy. I knew the kid wasn't bright, but I hadn't realized the true depth of his dimness. The suggestion that Buck would perform a heroic act and then wander off without giving his name was beyond comprehension. It was a wonder that Willy's folks let him out of the house unattended, he was such a sorry judge of character.

Suddenly, Willy, clutching the glass on the window, looked in the backseat. "Wow! What a neat twenty-two rifle! Can I shoot it sometime, Buck, can I? Ow! Ow!''

Buck rolled the window back down slightly to release Willy's fingers. "No, you can't shoot it! That gun's a classic. And you keep your grubby little grooved fingers off it!"

Buck said he would drop me at home, because he wanted to get over to the truck stop and make a move on the cute new waitress. I, on the other hand, was in the mood for a little adventure. "You got plenty of time for that, Buck. Why don't we just drive up Big Sandy and see if we can find Grogan?"

"You're as loony as Willy," Buck said. "Grogan can take care of himself."

"Yeah, but I was just thinking, if we did find Grogan, we'd be heroes, just like Willy said. Girls go for heroes in a big way. We might even get our pictures in the paper. Boy, would that ever impress that cute little waitress!"

Buck skidded the car to a stop, whipped it around in a bootlegger's turn, and, tires spinning on ice, headed back toward town. "Did I say we wasn't going to hunt for Grogan? I did not! A man can't let a lost person freeze to death and not make an effort to find him, even if that person is a sly old reprobate who would snooker the hide off you if you gave him the chance. You hear what I'm tellin' you?"

"Right, Buck."

On our way through town, Buck stopped by LeRoy's Truck Stop & Cafe to pick up a container of hot soup from the new waitress and to generally let it be known that he was on a heroic mission. Buck was smart that way. He liked to lay a bit of groundwork for his enterprises.

"You seem to be in a gosh-a-mighty hurry, Buck," LeRoy said.

"Got a man lost up on Big Sandy," Buck said. "Goin'
up there to find him before he freezes to death."

"Good gosh," said the cute, dimply waitress. A little tag
on her blouse identified her as Betty Lou. "That sounds
sooo dangerous, it being a blizzard and all. You be careful,
hear!"

"Yeah, Betty Lou," Buck said, using his Humphrey Bogart voice. "I'll be *real* careful. I ain't no stranger to danger,
sweetheart."

Now, there are few things a bunch of men sitting around
idle all day on a Sunday love more than going out on a
search for a lost person. Pretty soon LeRoy's customers were
leaping up and putting on mackinaws and hats and buckling
their pant legs into galoshes. Excitement had burst like a
small bomb in the café, and everyone talked at once.

"What's goin on?"

"Man lost up on Big Sandy."

"Better find him before he freezes to death."

"I'll go get my snowshoes."

"We may need some chains and shovels, too."

"Who is it, anyway?"

"Henry P. Grogan," Buck said.

The men took off their coats and sat back down. "More
coffee over here, Betty Lou."

I should explain here that Henry P. Grogan was the
tightest, shrewdest, connivingest old fraud of a businessman
in our entire town, possibly the state, and maybe the entire
universe. Stored in our basements, attics, garages, and barns
were enough rotten, rusty, mildewed, and worn-out pieces
of war surplus to outfit a small but unsuccessful invasion.
No one had ever come out on the better end of a deal with
Grogan.

"So it's old Henry P. got himself lost," LeRoy said. "Well, no matter. Here's the hot soup, Buck, just in case you find him. No charge. Don't let him drink too much of it right at first—might give him the cramps."

Back in the car and headed up to Big Sandy, Buck said, "Pop the lid off that soup and hand it to me." He then slurped down all the soup, thereby thoughtfully saving Grogan from any chance of getting the cramps. He wiped his mouth on his sleeve. "You see how that little cutie looked at me when she found out I was going out in a blizzard to search for a lost man?"

"Yeah. And I noticed you used your Bogart voice on her."

"Clark Gable. Worked like a charm, too."

Finding the lost man turned out to be a good deal easier than I expected. A couple of miles up Big Sandy, I spotted through the blizzard the dark shape of a man sitting on a log a hundred or so feet off the road. He was smoking a cigar. Buck and I jumped out and ran through the swirling snow. It was Grogan, all right. He puffed on his cigar and calmly watched us charging toward him. His ax and a little spruce tree leaned against the log beside him.

"Howdy, boys," Grogan said, beaming his snaggle-toothed grin. "You fellows out looking for a Christmas tree, too? Well now, I'm right sorry, but I probably cut the last decent little tree on this side of the mountain. Probably take you hours to find another one. But, what the heck, I could probably make you a deal on this fine tree."

"Ain't no tree I'm lookin' for," Buck said. "I'm lookin' for you, Henry P."

"Lookin' for me? What'd I do?"

"You got lost, that's what you did. And now I found you, so you ain't lost no more."

"I ain't lost no more and never been, you nincompoop. What ever gave you the idea I was lost? My car's just around the next bend in the road."

Buck glanced at me. "That's what they all say, lost people. See, he's already babbling out of his head from cold and hunger and hysterics. You're the witness!"

"Gee, Buck," I said. "I don't really think Mr. Grogan was ever really lo—"

"Shut up," Buck said, "and help me tote this here victim over to a warm car so we can revive him." He grabbed Grogan by the arm and began dragging the enraged little man through the snow.

"Leggo, you durn fool!" bellowed Grogan. "I don't want to go home yet! This is kidnapping!"

"Ain't neither. It's search and rescue. You been searched for and found, Henry P., and now you're being rescued. And you better come peaceful, 'cause if there's one thing I can't stand, it's an ungrateful victim. Now I want you to quit horsin' around and calm down, 'cause as soon as we get back to town we got to get our pitchers took for the newspaper."

"Pitchers took for the newspaper? How come?"

"Don't act dumb, Henry P. You know we're gonna get our pitchers took on account you got lost and I found you."

"Ha!" Grogan said. "I ain't gettin' my pitcher took!"

"Are so!"

"Ain't!"

"Listen, Henry P., if you don't go quietly, and admit to everybody I found you, then I'll never let you foist off on me any more of your rotten old war surplus junk." Buck had allowed a pleading tone to sneak into his voice, a big mistake. That was when the balance of power shifted from beef to brains. "Anyway, I already told all the folks down at LeRoy's truck stop you were lost and I was going to find you.''

"Now I get it,'' Grogan said. "You was down at the truck stop tryin' to get somethin' goin' with that cute little redheaded waitress. And usin' me for bait! Playin' the part of the big hero, wasn't you?''

"Could have been something like that,'' Buck admitted. "But it ain't gonna hurt you none to go along with it.''

"Oh, what the heck,'' Grogan said, smiling kindly. "We can probably work a deal.'' He turned to me. "Boy, fetch us that fine little Crimmas tree over here. Ain't that little tree about the purtiest one you ever seen, Buck? You understand, I can't really take money for lettin' you save me. Wouldn't be right. Keep me awake nights, frettin' over it. So we'll just do a little deal on that there tree.'' I went to get the tree, and so never heard exactly what deal they worked out. All I know is that Buck did a lot of yelling and arm waving.

After the picture-taking business at the newspaper, Buck and I drove Grogan back up Big Sandy to pick up his car. Then Buck took me home. As I was getting out, I noticed the little Christmas tree on top of the car. It made me laugh.

"How much did Grogan soak you for that tree?'' I asked.

"Just shut up and mind your own business,'' Buck snarled.

"Bet it was a lot. How much? Five dollars?''

Buck said a bad word and drove off.

Everything worked out about the way Buck planned. He and Grogan got their picture in the paper, with a story, and the headline that said LOCAL HERO SAVES CITY BUSINESSMAN. Buck did become a local hero briefly and got to date the cute little waitress, also briefly. Even with the brevity, I

figured she was worth five dollars, particularly if you considered that a fairly decent little Christmas tree was included
in the deal.

A short while later, I happened to stop by Grogan's War
Surplus and started sorting through his new used guns. It
was a hobby of mine. Also, I figured if I made a reasonable
purchase, I might wheedle out of Henry P. the terms of his
deal with Buck. Information like that can come in handy at
times.

"Don't touch the guns, boy!" Grogan shouted at me.
"How many times I got to tell you? Unless you got some
hard cash on you, of course. In which case, son, it's a whole
different matter."

"Well, I might have some hard cash," I said shrewdly.
"How much you want for this beaten-up rifle?"

"Ha! Ain't no way you got enough cash for that pump
twenty-two," he said. "That's a classic!"

Well, I knew all along it was a classic. It was just like my
cousin Buck's.

The Bust

Name's Joe Kelly. I'm a cop. Work out of Birders Enforcement, Seventh Precinct. It's a Saturday, 9:46 A.M. I stake out the house of a two-bit pickpocket and generic thief by the name of Sammy "the Dip" Wakowski. Miss my lunch break. No sign of Sammy for three hours. He's starting to get me steamed. I'm dining in my car on a cold burger and a hot Coke when I spot Sammy slinking down the sidewalk toward his house. He's wearing a gray tweed sports jacket, a tattersall shirt, and jeans. A pair of binoculars dangles from his scrawny neck. The sneaky rat! The binoculars probably don't even have lenses in them, if I know Sammy. And the guy calls himself a birder!

I get out and follow Sammy up his porch, shove him through the door.

"Ow, knock off the rough stuff, Kelly!" he yelps, brushing splinters off his shoulder. "I shoulda knowed it was you. Cripes, don't even give a guy a chance to open his door."

"Up against the wall, creepo," I say. "You know the posture." I pat him down. Seven wallets, thirty-nine credit cards, and a .45 automatic fall out of his coat. "Okay, Sammy, where is it?"

"Hey, I'm clean!"

"You can't fool me, Wakowski. Now trot it out before I forget my manners."

"What, for gosh sake?"

"Don't give me that, vacuum bag! You know darn good and well what I'm talking about—your life list!"

"My life list? How'd you know about my life list?"

"A little bird told me. Now where is it?"

"All right, all right, hold your horses. It's over on the bookshelf, that little book between *Do-It-Yourself Locksmithing* and the Audubon *Field Guide.*"

I walk over and grab Sammy's life list. It's a professional job, with a spiral wire binding, four-color cover. I flip through it. The name of each species is printed out, with spaces for the date and place of the spotting and another space for field notes. It's nice. And they say crime don't pay! My own life list is on matchbook covers and the backs of old envelopes and parking tickets. Just as I expected, nearly every species is filled in with Sammy's childish scrawl. This is a bogus life list if I ever seen one. Sure as God made pileated woodpeckers, Sammy's committed a Birders 904. I walk back and slam him into a chair by a table. I sit down and open the book.

Sammy takes the cigarette I offer him. He lights up, inhales deeply, nervously, blows a cloud of smoke at me. I smile and put the cigarettes back in my pocket. If I don't get Sammy one way, I'll get him another.

"Okay, Sammy, let's get down to it. How long you been keeping your life list?"

"Gee, I don't know, six months maybe. I picked the book up off a guy's desk. Didn't know what it was. Brand-new, still had the price sticker on it. All I had to see by was my little penlight. So I slipped the book in my pocket, what the heck. It's what you call compulsive stealing."

"Right," I say. "Now you mean to tell me you spotted all these species in six months?"

"Yeah. Well, it coulda been eight months, I ain't exactly sure."

"And you're telling me all these species on your list are legit?"

"Sure. I went out and personally watched every one of the feathered little buggers, yer robin, yer iggle, all like that."

"Iggle?"

"Yeah, yer bald-headed iggle. Big bird. Real big. Easy to spot."

"I see. Well, let's take the robin, for instance. Did you actually go out and look at a robin before you added it to your life list?"

"Hey, man, you kidding me? Of course not! Everybody's seen a robin, for cripes sake. It was rainin' the day I started my list. You think I'm gonna go out in the rain just to look for a lousy robin? I seen a million of 'em over the years. So I just took one robin from my past and wrote it in. Big deal!"

"Big deal is right. You violated six forty-seven of the Birders Code when you wrote in the date of robin spotting when you actually didn't spot a robin on that day nor had any intention of attempting to do so. I'm going to have to read you your rights." I read him his rights.

"That's all the rights I got?"

"Yeah, they're cutting down on them. Now let's see, you listed spotting a robin at a specific time and place when you in fact had not done so. Is that correct?"

"I guess. Listen, maybe I should call my lawyer. Okay, I admit I cut a few corners here and there on my life list. Hey, I ain't no kid. I get this life-list book here, I'm forty-seven years old. My life's half over, maybe a whole lot more than that, if I don't get some loan sharks paid off. So here I am, forty-seven years old, looking down at my life list, and all the spaces are blank. After a while, it starts to drive me crazy. You hear what I'm telling you, Kelly? I'm forty-seven years old and I ain't listed a single bird yet. My life seems like a total zero. I figure, what the hey, I deserve a handicap. I give myself fifty or so species, just to get started. Evens me out with the dude what started his life list when he was twelve years old. It's only fair. I didn't take all rare birds neither. Just tossed one in now and again. That should count for somethin'."

I stare at him. It makes me sick to my stomach, a guy pulling something like that with his life list. I flip through the book. "You're pretty stupid, Sammy. You indicate spotting all your phony species on one day."

"That's what you think. I wrote down different dates and places for all the birds I took for a handicap, just in case some cop come nosin' around. All those other birds you're talkin' about I spotted in one day."

"In Spokane? You're putting me on."

"Naw, really. They're legit. See, I'm visiting my sister in Spokane. They don't have much crime there, so I think maybe I'll import some. I'm lookin' around town, checkin' things out, and I drifts into this zoological museum place.

They got maybe a thousand birds in there. I whip out a pen
and paper and start writing them down to add to my life
list.''

"What you're telling me, you included on your life list
all these birds fluttering around in a big cage? That's a three
seventy-nine, listing caged birds. And you claim you knew
how to identify them all? No way, Sammy, no way!''

"It's true! And they wasn't fluttering around. They was
all dead. Hey, I see the way you're looking at me! I didn't
do it! They was dead when I got there, honest to God. And
each one had a little name tag on it. Helped out a whole lot
with identification, I can tell you that. Boy, if there's one
thing I hate, it's trying to find some jerky little bird in a
field guide while the little beast is hopping all over the place
and I got one eye in the binoculars and the other on the
field guide, which I'm flipping through like crazy! *And it's
never there!* I'll give you a tip, Kelly. Dead birds is the only
way to fly.''

"Get your coat, Sammy,'' I tell him. "I'm taking you
in.''

"What's the charge?''

"Cheating on your life list.''

"Okay, I'll go quietly. But first, let me stash these wallets.''

What a weirdo! What's one guy need with seven wallets?

Real Ponies
Don't Go Oink!

Even when we were small boys, Crazy Eddie Muldoon and I were gnawed by that terrible hunger known to nearly every boy in that distant time, the hunger for our very own pony to ride. We dreamed the impossible dream: on our next birthday, or surely the one after, we would awaken to hear our beaming parents gush, "Guess what's tied up out behind the woodshed, Son. But before you rush off to see what it is, you'd better open this present that's in the shape of a saddle." Sure enough, the present would be a saddle! Then you would tear out of the house and there, hidden behind the woodshed, probably with a big bow around its neck, would be your . . . very . . . own . . . pony! You would saddle up your pony and gallop off toward the horizon, pausing only long enough to wave at your generous and thoughtful and loving parents, the very best parents in the whole world.

My family wasn't big on impossible dreams. "Would you shut up about a pony!" my mother roared every time I brought up the topic. "Ponies cost money! You think money grows on trees?"

Occasionally, I would ride one of our pigs by the kitchen window, hoping to shame Mom into buying me a pony. "There goes old short-in-the-saddle," my sister, the Troll, would shout. "Hopalong Hog and Gene Oink, the smelly cowboy!" Then she and Mom would have a good laugh. Their response didn't leave me much hope of ever getting my very own pony by appealing to sympathy.

Crazy Eddie fared scarcely better. "Would you shut up about a pony!" Mr. Muldoon would roar. "Ponies cost money! You think money grows on trees?" Still, the Muldoons had an actual farm, with cows, sheep, pigs, chickens, rabbits, and even a goat, which, by the way, wasn't a bad ride. A pony would have fit right in to the Muldoon menagerie. If you stared hard enough at their pasture, you could easily imagine a pony out there. You could almost see it in fact, and one morning I *did* see it! Galloping majestically across the pasture was—forget the dumb pony—a beautiful, huge, glistening black horse!

Eddie was riding the horse.

It was almost too much for me to bear. True, Eddie didn't exactly fit my idea of a cowboy. The horse's back was so broad that Eddie's stubby legs stuck straight out on either side, as if he were doing an equestrian version of the splits. Eddie and the horse were totally out of aesthetic proportion to each other. From a distance, the two of them looked like a mouse riding a tall dog, although I knew the image would hurt Eddie's feelings.

"You look like a mouse riding a tall dog!" I called out to him.

Eddie galloped over, reined in right next to me, and glared down. He had to lean out precariously in order to see over the curve of the horse's barrel-shaped belly. "You're just jealous," Eddie said. "I bet you want a ride."

"Naw," I said. "I'm expecting my own pony any day now. I'll wait and ride it."

"If you climb up the barbwire and stand on top of that fence post, I'll pull you up," Eddie said.

"Okay," I said.

I climbed the post and Eddie hauled me up behind him. The view was wonderful from up there. You could see practically forever. The two of us rode off singing "Back in the Saddle Again," even though this was only our first time in the saddle. Our legs jutted straight out to the side, so there was no reason to argue about who got to use the stirrups. Actually, doing the splits while trotting about on horseback isn't nearly as painful as it sounds. Excruciating, yes, but scarcely more uncomfortable than that. Cowboys are tough.

It turned out that Old Tom, the horse, had recently been destined for another existence in the form of fox food. One of the farmers up the road raised foxes for their furs, and many a worn-out horse ended up there as the luncheon special. Apparently, the farmer had an excess of fox food for the moment and asked Eddie's father if he had use for a horse. Mr. Muldoon said he could probably think of one, if he put his mind to it.

Old Tom had already done a little time at the fox farm and, while exhausting the appeals process, had got religion.

He had been a bad horse, even a wicked horse, and his former owner had finally got fed up with his behavior and sent him up the road. His first week at the Muldoons, Tom was still figuratively wiping the sweat from his brow over his narrow escape from a career as fox food. You couldn't have asked for a sweeter, gentler horse for two little boys.

After a week or two, however, Old Tom apparently forgot his last-minute reprieve. He got it into his head that he had always lived at the Muldoon farm and, furthermore, probably owned it. He soon relapsed to his former nasty self. Hardly a day went by that he didn't buck us off. While we tried to get his bridle on he would casually place a hoof on one of my feet. Then he would put all his weight on that one hoof, balancing there, with daylight showing between the ground and his other three hooves. I would be yelling and thrashing about, and Tom would nonchalantly turn his head and look back, as if wondering what all the ruckus was about. Eddie would be trying to get the bridle over Tom's ears, and the horse would suddenly jerk his head up and send Eddie flying. Old Tom was wearing us out. He finally became so haughty he decided he didn't want to be ridden at all. Practically every day, carrying his bridle, we trailed Tom from one end of the farm to the other and back again, but almost never caught him. Then Eddie came up with the idea of roping the horse when it came to get a drink from the watering trough. First, though, we needed to find a rope.

Eddie's father had been putting a new layer of shingles on the barn and had bought a long rope that he tied to a big thick belt around his waist. He fastened the other end of the rope to a tractor, then climbed up a ladder and worked his way up over the steep roof of the barn to the far side, where the rope held him in place while he worked on the shingles. We found the rope neatly coiled by the tractor with the belt resting on top of the coil. Mr. Muldoon must have been taking a coffee break in the house, because he was nowhere in sight. Eddie looked this way and that, and then said he didn't think his pa would mind our using the rope to lasso Old Tom.

"I wish Pa was a cowboy or rancher, instead of just a farmer," Eddie said, grunting as he hoisted the big coil of rope and draped it over his shoulder. "Or a professional baseball player. That would be good. But he's just so ordinary. All he does is dumb things, like put new shingles on the barn. It's sort of embarrassing."

"Yeah," I said, trying to sound sympathetic, as though my family were interesting.

I suggested to Eddie that we cut off a piece of rope long enough for a lariat, but Eddie said no, it might make his pa mad. He said it would be better if we used the whole rope and just tied a loop in one end. He hauled all the rope out to the watering trough, tied a loop, and climbed up on the corral fence above the trough. The excess rope was scattered about the barnyard behind us in coils and assorted snarls.

Presently, Tom came moseying out of the pasture and headed for the trough. He stopped and eyed us suspiciously. Satisfied that he could handle anything we might have thought up for him, he plodded on in.

"What are you boys up to now?" growled Mr. Muldoon, coming behind us. Startled, we both jumped.

"Nothin', Pa," Eddie said. "Why?"

"Why! Well, because you got my new safety rope snarled all over the barnyard, that's why!"

"Sorry, Pa," Eddie said, turning his attention back to Tom. The horse was dipping its muzzle into the trough. "We're just trying to catch Old Tom."

"He's a lazy beast," Mr. Muldoon said. Both Eddie and

I were intently watching Old Tom. It was only much later that we learned Mr. Muldoon had picked up his safety belt and strapped it on. "I'd help you catch him, Son, but I got to get this barn shingled before it starts to rain."

"That's okay, Pa," Eddie said. "I think we just about got him."

Mr. Muldoon started untangling the safety rope and forming it into a coil on the ground.

Tom lifted his dripping muzzle from the trough and glared up at us, his ears flattened back against his head. Eddie tossed the lasso around his neck and jerked it tight.

The horse reared up, pawed the air, and whinnied angrily. Then it bolted for the pasture. The rope sizzled through Eddie's hands. "Ow!" he cried, jerking away. "That burns!"

"Now what's got into Old Tom?" Mr. Muldoon said, looking up from his coil of rope. "Stupid horse!"

"I lassoed him," Eddie explained.

"You did?" Mr. Muldoon said. "With wha—?"

All the loops and turns and tangles of rope slithered this way and that and then snapped straight out toward the pasture. The coil at Mr. Muldoon's feet disappeared like a giant strand of spaghetti slurped from a plate. At that instant Mr. Muldoon took the longest step I'd ever seen anyone take in my life. He must have stepped a good thirty feet from takeoff to touchdown. Both Eddie and I were impressed.

"Wow!" Eddie cried. "Did you see that! Holy smokes! And look at Pa go now! I never knew he could run so fast! He must be trying to help us catch old Tom!"

He sounded so pleased and proud that I couldn't help but envy him. Eddie obviously had the fastest father in the county, maybe in the whole country or even the world.

Old Tom must have been surprised, too, and even terrified, when he saw Mr. Muldoon racing after him at such amazing speed for a mere human. Tom kicked up his heels, stretched out, and ran even harder, as if his life depended on it, which, as we later learned, it did.

Eddie and I watched until his pa and Tom disappeared into the creek bottom, both of them practically flying. As far as we could judge, though, Mr. Muldoon wasn't gaining an inch on the horse.

"Shucks," Eddie said. "Pa ain't ever gonna catch Tom just by chasing him. He should know better. A horse can outrun a man every time, even one as fast as Pa."

"Hard to say," I said. "Your pa was really moving. I bet if he wasn't wearing his big ol' clodhopper boots he could."

"Maybe," Eddie said. "But there's no point in us waiting around for them to get back. We might as well go do something else. Got any ideas?"

"We could go ride your pigs," I said. "To tell you the truth, I'm kinda sick of horses."

"Yeah, me too," Eddie said. "So which pig you want to ride, Trigger or Champ?"

Blood Sausage

One crisp fall day, my stepfather, Hank, and Rancid Crabtree butchered one of our hogs. In those days, slaughtering and butchering were skills considered essential to survival on a small farm, and for that flimsy reason I had been ordered to participate in the ceremonies. It was common knowledge among my family and friends that I had a weak stomach, a stomach that would do back flips at the mere thought of butchering, let alone actually rummaging around inside a dead hog. On those grounds, I appealed to my kindly old grandmother to be excused from the nasty task.

"Stop that whinin' and bellyachin'!" Gram responded kindly. "Now git on out there and help with that butcherin'!"

"No! It'll make me deathly ill, I tell you! You can't force me to do this! Look, I'm already gagging. *Aaack! Aaack!*

You'll never forgive yourself if you make me do this and I gag to death.''

"Try me! Listen, you keep begging your ma and me to let you go hunting by yourself, right? So assuming we were crazy enough to let a twelve-year-old youngun without a bit of sense in his head wander off into the woods with a loaded rifle and assuming this youngun actually shot a deer, how is this youngun planning on dressing out this deer? Bring it home for his poor old granny to perform the chore?''

"Yeah, that was my plan. Why do you ask? You thinking about letting me go deer hunting?''

I always figured the reason God invented skin was so people like me wouldn't have to look at innards. Even though I carefully explained this theological concept to Gram, I was forcefully propelled out to the killing ground behind the barn to help with the butchering. My dog, Strange, already in cheerful attendance, danced about shouting his approval and applauding each grisly detail. There were few things Strange enjoyed more than a good butchering. He was the sort of dog that could be found munching popcorn in the front row at a public hanging.

For me, the butchering was just as awful as I had expected. Hank and Rancid didn't help much, either. Hank, a Frenchman, loved cooking exotic dishes, some of which you could actually stand to eat with your eyes open, as long as you didn't know the ingredients. Rancid, on the other hand, had the culinary aptitude of a coyote, and the table manners, too, come to think of it.

"Look here, Pat," Hank said. "A lot of folks don't think this thing right here is good to eat.''

"Aaaack!" I said. "A lot of folks are right, too!''

"Rancid, you eat this, don't you?'' Hank said.

"Shore, Hank, and it's right tasty, too, fried up with a little garlic and b'ar grease."

"Now you take these little morsels here, they're dang good eatin'," Hank said.

"*Aaaack!*" I said. "You're lying, Hank! You just say that to be disgusting and try to make me sick! *Aaaack!*"

"No, I ain't. You like these little morsels, don't you, Rancid?"

"Shore! They's might fine eatin', fried up with a little garlic and b'ar grease."

"You guys are pulling my leg," I said. "You're trying to make me sicker to my stomach than I already am. I suppose next thing you're going to tell me is that you saved that dishpanful of blood over there—*aaaack!*—because it's good to eat."

"Ah was wonderin' about thet mawsef, Hank," Rancid said. "How come you saved all thet blood?"

"To make blood sausage with, of course," Hank replied. "Nothin' like fried blood sausage with *grosses crêpes* on a cold winter morning. Mmmmm! Makes my mouth water just thinking about it."

"*Aaaack!*"

To the best of my recollection, that was the first and only time I ever saw Rancid gag. Even Strange looked a little queasy.

Blood sausage! Surely, I thought, Hank jests. But no, he fully intended to make blood sausage. Scarcely was the butchering finished than all members of the family were enlisted in the gory undertaking. I tried to make a break for it, but Gram snared me by an ear and dragged me back. My assignment was to stir the blood in a big pot on the stove.

"They must have laws against forcing a kid to stir blood," I said. "You probably could be arrested for this."

"You ain't no better than the rest of us," Gram growled. "Now shut up and stir that—*aaaack!*—blood!"

"I'll get you for this, Gram," I threatened. "You just wait and see if I don't!"

"You and who else?" Gram said with a chuckle, good-naturedly tweaking my ear into a figure eight. Gram was one of the fastest ear tweakers in the West, and not easily intimidated. "Now," she growled, "stir that pot of blood—*aaaack!*—like Hank told you to."

"Aaaack!" I replied, and started stirring the blood. Clearly, if I didn't assert myself in some way, Gram would continue to dominate me. I needed to show her that I couldn't be pushed around without retaliating. But what was her weak spot? Maybe Gilbert.

Gilbert had been my grandmother's boyfriend for several years. He was a tall, thin man, almost as shy as he was bald. He had an important and highly technical job in town, single-handedly operating the film projector at the Pandora, our only movie theater. I thought it had to be about the best job in the world, being a master movie projectionist. First of all, you got to see all the movies free and each one over and over. And then there was all the excitement and danger Gilbert told us about. Sometimes the film would break right at the climax of a movie, and Gilbert would have to calmly splice the film while the audience booed and hissed and some of the rowdier loggers threatened to integrate the faulty projector with the brave projectionist. "It takes nerves of steel," Gilbert told us one evening at dinner.

"Fascinating," Hank said. "Please pass the gravy."

"By the way, Hank, this dish is absolutely delicious,"

Gilbert said. "I've never tasted anything quite like it. What are these scrumptious little morsels?"

"Hog lips," I said. "Care for another helping, Gil?"

Gilbert's fork froze halfway to his mouth, but then Gram explained that I had just been joshing, and as soon as she laid hands on me my ears would be tweaked so hard I could use them for eye shades. Had I been so uncouth as to mention some of the actual ingredients in Hank's creation, Gilbert's entire body would have seized up right there at the dinner table. We would have had to carry him home in his chair, the fork still frozen halfway to his mouth.

Stirring the pot of blood on the stove, I recalled Gilbert's reaction to my little joke that evening. No doubt about it, Gilbert was the soft underbelly of my grandmother's defenses. That was where I would strike, should the opportunity present itself. As it happened, the opportunity presented itself much sooner than I expected.

Each member of the family had been assigned a task in the making of the blood sausage. Gram worked grimly at the kitchen table with a big butcher knife, chopping up garlic and onions and other ingredients. My sister, Troll, measured out the choppings and hauled them over to dump them in the cauldron that I stirred. Mom waited to begin her work of assisting in filling the sausage casings. Hank, as master chef, directed the whole operation.

Everything went smoothly, or as smoothly as the making of blood sausage can go. In the next to final step, Mom stood on one chair holding an empty sausage casing that dangled almost to the floor, and Hank stood on another chair, filling the casing with the loathsome concoction. The casing was tied off in sections to make links, which were then boiled. The boiled links actually looked pretty good, although no one present, except Hank, had any intention whatsoever of even sampling the blood sausage in his or her lifetime. Perhaps, I thought, I could get Gilbert to eat one of these sausages. Then I would tell him the major ingredient. I could say the whole thing was Gram's idea. Ha!

When we were almost finished, Gram, Troll, and I glumly watched Mom and Hank, up on their chairs, filling the final six-foot sausage casing. As the dark, disgusting liquid rose higher and higher, the casing bulged and glistened grotesquely. Then disaster struck. The casing burst! *KA-BLOOOOSH!* Blood flew in all directions, splashing to the floor and sweeping back and forth in ever-diminishing tidal waves. Soaked head-to-foot with blood, we stared at each other in stunned silence. Gram's face contorted with fury. She shook the big butcher knife at Hank and snarled, "Just look at the mess you've made of my kitchen! I knew something like this would happen!"

Then came the sound of the back door opening and closing and timid footsteps crossing the utility room to the kitchen.

"Hello," Gilbert called out. "Anybody home?" He stepped into the kitchen, carrying a bouquet of wildflowers in a little vase. "My goodness! What on earth? Is that . . . ?"

We were naturally all embarrassed to be caught in such a mess. It is very difficult to explain to a visitor how your kitchen and yourselves came to be covered with blood. Suddenly, I realized fate had thrust upon me the opportunity of a lifetime.

"Run for your life, Gil!" I yelled, pointing at Gram. "She's got a knife!"

The vase of wildflowers smashed to the floor. Ashen-faced, mouth agape, Gilbert backed away on rubbery legs.

"Wait, Gilbert!" Gram cried out. "Don't go!" She rushed toward him, reaching out to grab the hands he was weakly slapping at her. I suspect Gram's approach might have had a greater calming effect if she hadn't still been holding the big butcher knife.

We were all pretty startled by Gilbert's reaction. Finally, Hank, who had a great sense of humor, broke out in a chuckle. "Well," he said, "there goes old Nerves-of-Steel!"

Even Gram had to laugh, although not until the following week.

Troll said, "Wow! Did you see that! Wow!"

Mom said, "But what about my screen door?"

Hank said, "Oh, don't worry about that. Gil probably dropped it in the driveway."

Gram later tracked Gilbert down and explained the situation to him, that we had been canning raspberries and a jar had burst. Gil said he knew it was a joke right from the beginning and had gone along with it just for the fun. He said he liked to play the clown on occasion. "Sorry about the screen door."

A few nights afterward he was at our house for dinner.

"What's wrong with your ear, Pat?" he asked me.

"Oh, it's just recovering from a bad tweaking," I said. "Nothing serious. When it grows back on, it'll be good as new."

"Have another sausage, Gil," Hank said. "Made it myself."

"Don't mind if I do," Gilbert said. "It's delicious! Can I get the recipe?"

"You bet," I said. A tweaking should not go unavenged.

Crash Dive!

Let me see if I can still remember the proper sequence of events, which in some small way may have contributed to Mr. Muldoon's peculiar behavior that wonderful, glorious summer after third grade. First, I had narrowly escaped drowning in the diving bell Crazy Eddie Muldoon and I had built out of an old milk pail, a hose, and a tire pump. Some kind of technical problem, as I recall.

Next, the bush plane we built on top of the Muldoon barn crashed on takeoff. Eddie was pilot and I, copilot. Eddie claimed the crash was a result of wind shear or some such thing. I thought it was pilot error, but never expressed my opinion to Eddie, nor to the board of inquiry that investigated the crash. ("What in the name of heaven were you two . . . !")

Then we dug the pit trap for capturing wild animals in

the Muldoon pasture. All we managed to capture, however, were a small but nervous skunk and Mr. Muldoon,
unfortunately both of them at the same time. We tried to
explain to Eddie's father how lucky it was that he had landed
in the trap with a mere skunk rather than, say, a mountain
lion, which was what we had hoped to catch. A mountain lion
could have torn him to bits, whereas the skunk smell wore
off him in less than a year. It is difficult, however, to get a
grown-up to pay attention to two eight-year-old boys, no
matter how sensible they may be, and Mr. Muldoon was
no exception.

It was during the course of the above-mentioned ventures
that I observed Mr. Muldoon's behavior becoming increasingly strange and unpredictable. For example, Eddie and I
would be doing nothing more than pulling a little wagonload
of boards across the yard, when Mr. Muldoon would pop
out of the barn and yell something irrational at us, like,
"Stay out of my workshop! Don't touch my tools! Don't
build nothin'!" To me, he seemed to be getting weirder and
weirder with each passing day. I didn't mention this to
Eddie, however, because I didn't want to distract him from
our Top Secret Project—the design and construction of a
submarine.

The work on the submarine was top secret, because,
Eddie said, he wanted to surprise his parents. That was one
of the nice things about Eddie—he was always thinking up
new ways to surprise his parents. That may be why both
his mother and father went about with constant surprised
looks. It was sort of eerie, actually. Eddie's parents were
beginning to make me uneasy, with all their twitches and
jerks, surprised looks and irrational shouting.

Eddie and I worked on the submarine every chance we

got. As soon as his father had gone off on his tractor to plow
a field or something, we would rush into his workshop and
grab armfuls of tools and haul them off to the building site.
Eddie explained to me that when his father said "Don't
touch my tools!" he didn't really mean "Don't touch my
tools!" but something else.

"What else?" I asked.

"I'm not sure," Eddie said, selecting a saw and testing
it for sharpness with his thumb. "Just something else. Why
do you ask?"

"No reason. You think we'll need the brace-n-bit today?"

"Yes. And fill your pockets with those big nails. We'll
need lots of nails."

Much of our time was spent scouring the countryside for
submarine-building materials, which were fairly scarce in
North Idaho. Nevertheless, we salvaged numerous boards
from an old shed Mr. Muldoon probably was planning on
tearing down anyway. We also had the good fortune to find
an old wooden barrel, an abandoned hog trough, a washtub,
several lengths of stovepipe, some metal roofing, a hose, a
tire pump, a truck inner tube, and various other essentials
of submarine construction.

Slowly the sub took shape. The long sleek hull contained
hatches fore and aft, for quick departures from the deck
prior to crash dives. A four-inch swivel gun was mounted
just ahead of the forward hatch. The conning tower jutted
magnificently up from the deck, its side painted with the
name of our deadly underwater craft—*Sea Wuff*. The very
name sent chills up and down our spines.

Eddie designed and manufactured the periscope himself.
In many ways it was the most impressive part of the sub-

marine. Several small mirrors of the kind mothers and sisters carry in their purses were cleverly mounted inside a tube in such a way that it was possible to run the periscope up from the conning tower, peer into the lower opening, and see an eye staring back.

The first time I looked through the periscope I shouted at Eddie, "Crash dive! Crash dive! There's an eye bearing down on us at twenty knots!"

Eddie was not amused, and I narrowly escaped court-martial.

We made several trial runs with the sub and everything worked perfectly. It slithered silently as a shark's ghost beneath the unsuspecting enemy, entered and left harbors of the world undetected, and scouted the far reaches of the Pacific and Atlantic. Satisfied with its performance, Captain Crazy Eddie Muldoon decided that at last the time had come to subject our submarine to the ultimate test—putting it in actual water.

With the foresight of any good engineer, Eddie had built the submarine on top of two round fence posts. Eddie stationed himself in the conning tower during the launch, so that he could direct the crew in the proper method of pushing the submarine into water. The crew put its shoulder to the stern of the sub, pushed, and the vessel slid into the waves to the resounding applause and cheers of the captain and crew. The crew then leaped aboard, almost ejecting the captain from the conning tower, and once again narrowly escaping a court-martial. The sub soon righted itself. Scarcely had it done so, however, than the crew detected what it supposed to be a serious flaw in the craft.

"It's sinking!" the crew yelled. "It's sinking!"

"It's supposed to sink, you fool," the captain snarled at the crew. "It's a submarine!"

Not being stupid, the crew chose that moment to mutiny and leaped back toward shore, sinking over its sneakers into black muck.

The *Sea Wuff* drifted aimlessly about, its deck spouting fountains of water from every orifice, of which there were a good many. The captain, however, showed no sign of abandoning the conning tower. Indeed, his attitude reflected nothing less than sublime confidence. He gripped the conning-tower rail and stared down at the deck of the craft settling into the murky waves beneath him.

"Go get my folks," he ordered the crew presently. "I want them to see this. It'll be a big surprise for them."

The crew, not at all sure the captain hadn't gone totally mad, raced across a field, over a fence, through the barnyard, over the lawn, and burst into the kitchen, where Mr. and Mrs. Muldoon were just sitting down for an afternoon coffee break.

"Quick!" the crew shouted. "The sub's about to crash dive."

Mr. Muldoon had just taken a bite of cinnamon toast, a piece of which protruded from his trembling lips. The entire left side of his face convulsed in a gigantic twitch. As I say, the man was strange.

"S-sub?" he said. "What's a sub?"

"Crash dive?" Mrs. Muldoon said. "What's a crash . . . ?"

"SUBMARINE!" roared Mr. Muldoon. *"SUBMARINE!"* He leaned forward, grabbed the suspenders of the crew's overalls, and jerked them up to within an inch of his face. *"WHERE? WHERE? THE CRICK? THE LAKE? WHERE?"*

He scared the crew so badly for a moment it couldn't remember where the submarine was crash diving. Besides

that, he had sprayed cinnamon-toast crumbs in the crew's
eyes. Finally, the crew was able to blurt out, "The d-d-d-
d-d-duck pond!"

Mr. and Mrs. Muldoon fairly exploded out the door and
raced each other across the lawn, through the barnyard,
over the fence, and across the pasture. "Cripes," the crew
said to itself. "You'd think they'd never seen a submarine
crash dive before." Not wishing to be left out of the surprise, however, the crew sped after the Muldoons and arrived at the duck pond mere seconds behind them. They
slid to a stop and stood wheezing and gasping at the pond's
edge, staring out at what no doubt to them appeared to be
nothing more than an old wooden barrel protruding from
the water. From the interior of the conning tower, for that
in fact was the true nature of the barrel, came an ominous
sound.

Wush-wush-wush-wush-wush-wush.

"Eddieeee!" screamed Mrs. Muldoon.

Crazy Eddie's head popped up out of the barrel. "Hi,
Ma. Pa. What do you think of the submarine?"

Mr. Muldoon flopped down on his seat and stared out at
his son, the captain of the *Sea Wuff*.

"What in heck are you doing out there?" he croaked,
swabbing the sweat from his face with a grungy old bandanna.

"Well, after my cowardly crew mutinied, I crash dived
to the bottom. Now I'm surfacing again."

"Surfacing," Mr. Muldoon said, studying the sleek hull
beneath the lapping waves. "Good luck."

"Thank you, sir," the captain said, and disappeared back
into the barrel.

Wush-wush-wush-wush-wush-wush-wush-wush.

We then observed one of the great miracles of modern technology. Slowly, wobbly but steadily, the submarine began to rise to the surface. Eddie's calculations had proved correct. It was indeed possible for him to inflate with a hand pump the truck inner tube installed directly below the conning tower.

Mr. and Mrs. Muldoon were wonderfully surprised and even cheered and applauded this display of well-known American ingenuity. As they strolled limply back toward their house, Mr. Muldoon suddenly stopped, appeared to think for a moment, then spun around.

"Tire pump!" he shouted. "What's my tire pump doing out in the middle of a duck pond? Where did you get the inner tube? My tools!"

Later that summer, the Muldoons moved away and I never again saw Crazy Eddie, the pal with whom I had first skinned my knees, blackened my eyes, bloodied my nose, and broken my bones, the ties that truly bind. My mother, grandmother, and I went over to bid the Muldoons goodbye. Crazy Eddie stood straight and fairly tall on the back of the old flatbed truck that was loaded down with all the Muldoon furniture. As the truck pulled out of the yard, he threw me a jaunty salute, turned, stared straight ahead, and never looked back. I sadly watched my friend vanish into a future we would not share, the heavy silence broken only by the sounds of Mom and Gram leaping into the air and clicking their heels.

My Abduction by Creatures From Space, for What It's Worth

I just read a nonfiction book by an author who was kidnapped by aliens from space and taken aboard their flying saucer, where he was subjected to a variety of experiments and then returned safely to his own bed, none the worse for wear but with a bad case of the nerves and an idea for a best-seller. According to the book, such abductions by aliens are a fairly common occurrence, something I hadn't realized. Otherwise, I would have come forward much sooner and reported my own kidnapping by aliens. I had assumed my experience was unique, and so bizarre that people would poke fun at me or even suggest that the strange encounter was due to a bad batch of my elderberry wine, which, to tell the truth, was what I first suspected. But the haunting question remains: What would elderberry wine be doing with a spacecraft?

Although my abduction by aliens occurred on the night

of October 3, 1978, the incident is still fresh in my mind today. Indeed, it ranks right up near the top of my memorable experiences. I had gone up to my cabin on the river for a few days of relaxation and a little fishing. About nine o'clock, I set my North Idaho burglar alarm, which, when tripped, plays a recording of a shell being jacked into the chamber of a 12-gauge shotgun, a much more effective alarm than some silly beeping or clanging. I then enjoyed a glass of my latest batch of elderberry wine, and, much relaxed, went off to bed. About midnight, I suddenly awoke in a cold sweat, sensing the presence of something in the room with me. I am a little vague about the exact time, because when I sense an unknown presence in my room at night I tend to be somewhat lax in accumulating data that might later be of interest to scientific investigators. Therefore, when I say ''about midnight'' I mean anywhere from eleven P.M. Tuesday to four A.M. Friday. I was at first particularly disturbed by the extreme darkness of the room, which made it impossible to see anything, even though my room is equipped with a night light for medicinal purposes. Then I realized that the darkness was the result of my eyes being squeezed shut. Against my better judgment, I opened them.

A creature no more than three feet tall was standing in the corner of the room watching me. It had a deathly pale face, an O-shaped mouth, and two enormous eyes. (Quite likely, the creature had the same impression of me.) It was equipped with the normal number of arms and legs—no great comfort. Its body appeared to be covered with aluminum foil that gave off a mild iridescent glow. The creature moved toward me, its legs tight together as though tied by invisible bonds. Suddenly, although I heard nothing, a raspy voice sounded inside my head.

"Quick, where's your bathroom?" the voice said.

I pointed to the bathroom door. The creature rushed inside with the same jerky motion, and returned a few minutes later, walking normally.

"Whewee!" the voice said inside my head. "Long way between rest stops in this part of the galaxy. So, Crawford, I imagine you're wondering what I'm doing here in your bedroom at this hour of the night. My orders are to take you up to our spaceship, where a few minor experiments will be run on you. Afterward, we'll replace your skin and no one will ever guess you've been out of it. First of all, though, I'd better write 'front' and 'back' and 'this side up' on you, just as a precaution. We're advanced, but not all that advanced."

"Wait! Wait!" I shouted. "You've got the wrong guy! My name's not Crawford!"

"That's what they all say." The creature signaled toward the door, and in trooped a dozen tiny beings dressed as stevedores and grumbling about working overtime on regular pay. They held their bony little hands over me and I floated up into the air, a rather pleasant sensation, although I didn't fully appreciate it at the time. The next thing I knew I was hovering a few feet over a little clearing in deep woods. Creature voices crackled in my head:

"Where's the spaceship?"

"I told you this was the wrong direction, you idiot!"

"No, I'm right! The sun rises in the north and sets in the south."

"But this is Earth! Different sun!"

"Oh, I forgot. Must be mag lag. Takes me a day or two to get oriented. So, we're lost, guys. Anybody know what side of the trees the moss grows on? Hey, nobody panic! Maybe the human can help us find the ship. Listen, Crawford, don't just float there with that stupid look on your face. Help us out. We parked the ship next to a little pond in the woods near your cabin."

"Why should I help you find your ship?"

"Ever read in the tabloids about a guy who woke up with his skin on backward?"

"Just asking. The pond's over there."

A few minutes later, we were beneath the spacecraft, which was shaped like a saucer and about the size of Pittsburgh. Either that or it was shaped like Pittsburgh and about the size of a saucer. I was getting confused.

"What happens now?" I asked. "Are you going to beam us up?"

"No," the head creature replied. "We're advanced, but we're not all that advanced. Hey, somebody up there send down the ladder!"

Upon arriving at the top of the ladder, I entered a large circular room. A number of creatures leaned against the wall, looking bored. The floor was cluttered with dirty clothes and old pizza boxes. Loud, raucous music pounded from overhead speakers. I assumed this was the area of the spacecraft inhabited by teenage creatures.

The head creature, whom I'll call Ralph, took my hand and led me into a room I guessed was a nursery. Large, cream-colored larvae of some sort squirmed inside glass jars. It was hideous. I shuddered.

"What's wrong?" Ralph said. "You never seen fish bait before? The kids always bring their own grubs. Works great on your largemouth bass."

Ralph next led me into a room equipped with what looked like an operating table. He told me to climb up on the table. I viewed this as a bad omen, but my will to resist had been neutralized, either by telepsychic manipulation or Ralph's breath. I climbed up on the table. Presently, I was approached by an ancient creature that somehow gave me the impression of a praying mantis moonlighting as a bag lady. Whether the creature was male or female, I couldn't say, nor was it something I considered worth dwelling on at the moment. Maybe after a few decades in space, yes, but not sooner.

"Ah, Crawford, the chosen one!" the ancient thing growled inside my head. "It is you to whom we have brought the single greatest secret of the universe. You will go on what you call your television and make this secret known to all humans, so that they will be raised to the highest form of consciousness. For this service, you will be rewarded with wealth beyond even your imagination. You will know unbelievable luxury, Crawford, and . . . Please, allow me to call you by your first name. What is it? My memory is so bad!"

"Pat. Pat Crawford. So what's the single greatest secret of the universe?"

"It is just this. That the . . . uh, the uh . . . Let's see, how does that go? Darn this memory of mine! I should have written it down. It has totally slipped my mind! We're advanced . . ."

"Yeah, I know, but not all that advanced."

"The single greatest secret of the universe is a rather good joke, too, if I could just remember how it went. I think you would have enjoyed it. Oh well, we might as well do the usual skin thing with you. No sense in wasting a good specimen."

"Wait! Wait!" I shouted. "I'm not Crawford!"

All at once, I sat up. I was back safe and sound in my

own bed. But all I could see was darkness. I thought my
skin had been put on backward! Then I realized my eyes
were still closed.

Questions remain. Was I really dreaming? Was I in a
drunken stupor from elderberry wine? Had I momentarily
gone insane? If the creatures had actually entered the house,
why hadn't the burglar alarm gone off? Why why why? I
thought perhaps my friend Paul, the psychologist, could
put me into a deep hypnotic trance and extract the truth
from my subconscious. Paul was more than willing to hyp-
notize me, but later said there wasn't anything in my subconscious worth reporting on, and much of it was in bad
taste anyway. The only odd thing about the session was that
upon coming out of the trance I was possessed by a terrible
compulsion to pay Paul the twenty bucks I owed him on a
fishing bet. Was this some perverse trick of the creatures
from space? Questions! Questions!

Phantom of the Woods

When I was a boy, I generally adhered like glue to the laws of fishing and hunting. This was due to my keen sense of Truth, Honor, Duty, and Sneed.

Sneed was the local game warden, a person of mysterious powers that enabled him to materialize any time of the day or night at the very instant of a game violation. True, some people did get away with violating the fish and game laws, but Sneed prevented them from enjoying the transgression. They would scurry toward home with their illegal catch, jumping at every snap of a twig, breaking into a cold sweat at every rustle of grass, and swiveling their heads to catch sight of any shadow that seemed ready to pounce on them. In all honesty, I must admit that had it not been for Sneed, my sense of Truth, Honor, and Duty might have been a good deal less keen.

Sneed. Even now the sound of that name sends chills rippling down the highways and byways of my nervous system much as it did forty years ago. Once, Retch Sweeney and I, fourteen years old, were fishing a remote section of Sand Creek so early that dawn was but a sliver of milder darkness in the east. No sane adult would be out and about at such an hour, in such a place. We were catching big fat red-bellied cutthroat as fast as we could bait our hooks. Gripped as we were by a catching frenzy, the trout limit seemed a remote abstraction, a vague and boring notion we had once heard mentioned in our presence but scarcely the sort of thing to intrude upon the excitement of the moment. In the darkness behind us, unknown numbers of fish flopped happily about on the gravel.

"What's our limit?" I asked Retch, chuckling.

"All we can catch plus one fish," Retch said.

I lobbed another worm-laden hook out into the watery darkness swirling beyond the gravel bar, even as I detected a momentary chill in the air, as though a ghost had floated by, close enough to awaken the hairs on the back of my neck. Retch, too, had noticed the chill. We glanced about, seeking shape and substance for the invisible horror.

"Sneed," Retch croaked. "I know it's Sneed. He's out there someplace, watching. I can feel his eyes burning into my . . ."

And then we saw him—a shadow emerging from the mist, shaped like a man in a big hat and a long coat, gliding over the gravel of the bar as silently as if it were moss. Sneed! Cripes!

"Howdy, boys. You up a mite early today. Looks to me like you been havin' some fine luck."

"Y-yes, sir," Retch said. "Some good, some bad."

"Reckon I know what you mean," Sneed said. "You boys know how many fish you caught?"

"Not exactly," I said. "I'd guess we're pretty close to the limit, though."

"Right. But which side? The under side or the over side?"

He had me there. I never was much good at puzzles, particularly while quaking in my tennis shoes.

"Don't know, do you, boys? Well, let me put it this way. If each of you had caught one more fish, I would've had to take you in."

Take us in? The dreaded Sneed, *take us in!* We would have vanished from the face of the earth, never to be seen or heard of again. Two fairly innocent boys, sucked into oblivion. And for what? Two lousy fish over the limit!

"Actually, I was a little surprised to run into you two out here this hour of the morning," said the game warden. "I was really hoping to catch that rascal Rancid Crabtree. If you happen to see him, you might tell him that I'm checking these parts fairly often these days—and nights. Try to keep it in mind yourselves."

Then Sneed was gone in a swirl of mist, leaving a few boot prints on the gravel, almost as if he were human.

Retch and I collected our fish. Sneed had miscounted; we were each still several fish shy of the limit. "No point in being greedy," Retch said loudly, smoothing down the hairs on the back of his neck. "No point in always trying to catch the limit, that's what I always say."

"Right," I shouted. "That's what I always say, too."

On the way home, we stopped by Rancid Crabtree's shack, fired up his barrel stove, and put a pot of coffee on to boil. As always, the old woodsman was delighted to see us.

"Golllll-dang! What's the idear bargin' in here this hour the mornin', distarbin' a man's sleep?" Because Rancid's normal voice was a high-pitched squeal accomplished with little or no movement of his lips, someone meeting him for the first time might easily have jumped to the conclusion the man was agitated. Nothing could have been further from the truth. "Golllll-dang," he squealed between his teeth, throwing off his blankets. "You fellas eat a man out of house and home fer he's even outta bed."

"We brought you some fish," I said, nibbling on a hard, cold biscuit.

"Ah got fish," he said, yawning, combing his hair back with his fingers.

"I bet," I said. "That's what brought us by here this morning. Sneed caught us down on the crick. Scared the daylights out of us."

"You let ol' Sneed catch you?" Rancid said, cackling. "Thet's the funniest thang Ah heard today."

"He let us go, though."

"Noooo. Sneed let you go?"

"We were still a few fish short of our limit. But he told us to warn you."

"Warn me?"

"Yeah," Retch said, filling three grimy mugs with coffee. "He said, 'Tell Crabtree I'm gonna be out and about these parts and on the lookout for him and if I catch him violating any fish and game regulations I'm gonna nail his hide to my barn wall and tan it.' Ain't that about what he said, Pat?"

"Pretty near," I said. "Sneed's out to get you, Rancid."

"Haaaaaaaw! Ol' Sneed thanks he can nab me? Wahl, he got another thank comin'! They don't call me Phantom of the Woods fer nothin'!"

"Yeah, I guess not," I said. "Got any sugar for this coffee, Phantom?"

The following winter, Rancid and I were ice fishing on Pend Oreille Lake. The game regulations, according to Earl Pitts, said we could catch perch, kokanee, and whitefish through the ice, but we had to release any trout. We had both already caught and released several smallish rainbows.

A dozen or so other ice fishermen were scattered about the lake in our vicinity, but otherwise the great expanse of ice was empty. There was absolutely no way the game warden could approach without one of the ice fishermen spotting him and sounding the warning: "Sneed's coming. Pass it along."

The general concern about Sneed didn't mean that we were a bunch of deliberate law breakers. What it meant was, almost nobody ever sat down and actually *read* the fish-and-game regulations. It worked like this. You might ask Fred Jones what the limit on whitefish was. Jones might say, "Ain't none." How do you know, Fred? "'Cause Pete Wilson told me." How did Pete know? Sam Miller had told him. And so on. You assumed that somewhere back at the beginning of this chain of information, there was someone who had actually *read* the regulations. But you could never be sure. You yourself didn't want to read the regulations, because they gave you a headache. That was why it was necessary to keep a lookout for Sneed—headaches.

Rancid had considerable success that winter trapping skunks. The phrase "smell of success" was perhaps never more accurately descriptive than when applied to Rancid, and this explained why no fishermen were situated downwind of us. These were the circumstances that played right into Sneed's hands.

As we hunched over our little holes in the ice, with clouds

of snow whipping around us, Rancid suddenly shouted, "Gol-dang! Ah got a biggun on!" After much thrashing and splashing, he hauled out a twenty-inch rainbow trout. He removed the hook and laid the trout on the ice.

"Wow, what a beauty!" I said. "That's the nicest fish I've seen all year. Too bad you have to throw it back, Rancid."

The old woodsman stared at me, then down at his fish. He turned his head about, checking this way and that, trying to peer through the gusts of snow.

"I said, Rancid, *too bad you have to throw it back!*"

"Oh, Ah suppose so," he said. He picked up the trout and held it out toward the hole in the ice. "C'mon, fish, leggo maw hand! Ah said, leggo maw hand! Git back in thet water! Wahl, dadgumit, if you ain't got gumption enough to wiggle out of maw hand, you can jist go home with me. Ah ain't gonna force you to jump back in thet icy water if you don't want to!"

"Better toss it back, Rancid," I said.

"Haaaww!" he said. "This hyar fish don't want to be tossed back, do you fish? You wants to be snuck home and et by the Phantom, ain't thet right, fish?"

Ignoring what the fish might have to say, I peered off into the gusting snow. "I've got some bad news for you, Phantom. Here comes Sneed."

I wasn't fooling either. For a brief moment, I had glimpsed the shadowy form of a tall man gliding toward us through the billowing snow, approaching on our downwind side, which was unprotected by an early-warning system.

"You joshin' me?" the Phantom said.

"No!" I said. "But there's still time to toss the fish back."

"You better not be lyin'!" Rancid said. He moved to

toss the fish back, but then stopped. "No! Ah jist cain't do it. It ain't natural to throw back a fish this big!" And with that, he opened up his coat, stuffed the fish inside his shirt, and buttoned his coat back up.

Then Sneed was on us. "Howdy, men. Like to check your fishing licenses. See you got a nice catch of whitefish there. Ain't no limit on whitefish this year. Catch all you want. I suppose you know you got to throw any trout back, though. You know that, don't you, Crabtree?"

"Shore," Rancid said. But then, to Sneed's and my amazement, the Phantom hunched slightly over and burst out in a shrieking giggle totally unbecoming a grown man. With obvious great effort, Rancid cut the giggle short.

The game warden and I stared at the old woodsman with considerable concern. His whole chest was fluttering violently beneath his coat!

"You all right, Crabtree?" the game warden asked. "Ain't got a heart problem, have you?"

"Ah'm fine, fine!" Rancid then let out a whoop that caused Sneed and me both to jump back. The fluttering had now moved down in the direction of the woodsman's lower anatomy. Rancid clutched his belly with both hands and began to dance wildly about, alternately whooping and giggling and working in an occasional shrill burst of cussing.

"What you got under your coat there?" Sneed asked, his brow furrowing with suspicion.

"A big bananner fer maw lunch," Rancid lied. "Jist a big bananner."

"Well, that's the liveliest banana I ever seen," Sneed growled.

"Ain't it though," Rancid said.

Sneed folded his arms and, appearing much less con-

cerned, watched as Rancid struggled to control the fluttering
and thrashing that now slid slowly down his pant leg.

Then the trout squirted out of the pant leg onto the ice.
The three of us stared down at the big flopping rainbow.

"Praise be!" Rancid shouted. "It's a miracle! A bananner turned into a fish!"

Sneed was already writing out a ticket, using my back as
a desk. He handed the ticket to Rancid. "That trout just
cost you twenty-five dollars, Crabtree."

"Twenty-five dollars!" Rancid squealed. Then he turned
to me and asked, "How many skonks you reckon thet is?"

"I reckon about all the skunks in Idaho," I said. "But
they probably won't let you pay the fine with skunks."

"Wahl, hold on jist a dang minute, Sneed. Ah don't
thank Ah was actually breakin' the law. Ah was jist war-
min' thet fish up before tossin' it back in the icy water,
so . . ."

But Sneed had vanished, leaving a couple of boot prints
in the snow, almost as if he were human. The Phantom of
the Wood and I stood there thinking about Truth, Honor,
Duty, and Sneed. Then we packed up our whitefish and
headed home.

The Piano Lesson

My wife, Bun, sprang breathlessly through the door, slammed it shut, and, not satisfied with engaging the lock and dead bolt, pressed her shoulder hard against it. Upon regaining the power of speech, she shouted out that the garage had attacked her.

"What utter nonsense!" I exclaimed. "There's no way the garage would attack you. It's harmless. You may have startled it into making a threatening gesture or two, but true garage attacks are virtually unheard of."

"Oh yeah? How about the time the Sweeneys' garage ate Retch's dog, old Smarts?"

Bun had a point. I myself had witnessed Retch Sweeney's garage gobble up the inaptly named canine. Smarts, shuffling along too close to the open maw of the garage, had been slurped in, leaving only a surprised yelp hanging in the air. The dog was burped up a few minutes later, none the worse for wear, and no brighter, but with a haunted look on his face. The dog went about for days afterward telling of the horrors he had experienced in the labyrinthine innards of the Sweeney garage, but who's going to believe a stupid dog?

"Well, sure," I said. "A garage might gobble up a dumb animal but not an intelligent human being."

"In that case, both you and Retch are at considerable risk."

"Ha!" I shot back.

Speaking of garages, back when I was a young boy I knew a man who actually kept his car in one. His name was Mr. Jefferies. I don't know where he kept his boat and motor and canoe and tent and fishing tackle and all the other stuff usually stored in garages. Maybe he didn't own any. He never worked at a job, at least one that anyone knew about, because he went to the library almost every day. Miss Higgens, our town librarian, said she enjoyed checking books in and out for him, because it was nice to have someone around occasionally, to break the monotony. She said Mr. Jefferies knew how to read and speak French, too. Because of that some folks thought Mr. Jefferies might be a Communist saboteur, even though there wasn't anything around for him to sabotage, except Gus Dreeper's sawmill, which Gus said he wouldn't mind having blown up one dang bit anyway, as long as he had a bit of warning.

Actually, Mr. Jefferies wasn't all that interesting. I probably wouldn't even remember him except that he kept his car in his garage and later turned out to be totally insane. He also did me a wonderful favor. He ran off with Miss Swartz, my piano teacher. That's how I knew he was insane. A man would have to be crazy to run off with Miss Swartz.

My mother bought the piano for next to nothing from the Gregorys, a frail old couple whose farm the bank had foreclosed on. The Gregorys were going to try to make it to California in their old truck to pick fruit for a living, which seemed like a lot of fun to me, and I wished I had been going along, particularly when I found out Mom's intention for the piano. As it was, I had no way of knowing the piano had any connection with me. I assumed Mom had bought it only for some decorative purpose, possibly to cover up the spot where a leak in the roof had stained the wallpaper. Without warning I was signed up for piano lessons with Miss Swartz. Right to the last I was deceived. Mom said Miss Swartz would give me some culture. I thought it was something to eat, like custard. Piano lessons were the worst thing that ever happened to me. Thus did I become aware of the existence of evil in the world.

I didn't mind going to a piano lesson so much while school was on, because my day had already been ruined. When you're suffering anyway, another pain more or less doesn't make much difference. What I truly hated was piano lessons during my summer vacations. A lesson tainted an otherwise joyous day. It was like eating a fine crisp juicy apple that you know contains a worm. My first lesson came on just such a fine crisp juicy apple of a summer day. I was hollered in off the creek and made to take a bath, wash my hair, cut and clean my fingernails, and put on my good pants and my good shirt, all of which coming in a single day would have been too much to bear, except I was venturing into the unknown, which for me has always posed the possibility of adventure. I pedaled my bike off toward town and Miss Swartz's. So far so good.

About half a mile from town, I sighted Buster Cogwheel headed my way. Buster had a build like a short brick out-

house and about as many brains. I had heard on the grape-
vine that Buster was looking for me. He apparently had
some notion that I had stolen his canoe, which he kept hidden down on the creek so that the real owners couldn't find
it. How Buster had got such a ridiculous idea in his head I
don't know. First of all, as I had told my friends, I wasn't
in the habit of stealing, and had I been, I certainly wouldn't
have stolen from Buster, who had spotted me by now and
rushed to the center of the road, his arms spread wide to
nab me. Aware of the folly of attempting to reason with a
Cogwheel, I speeded up, hoping I would have enough momentum to run over him. This maneuver might have suc-
ceeded had I been driving a pickup truck but it was no good
on a bike.

The impact scarcely caused Buster to blink. He dragged
me from the bike by the neck and stood me up on the edge
of the pavement. I thought this might be a good time to try
reasoning with him, but before I could collect my wits he
punched me in the nose and sent me sprawling down into
the muddy ditch.

"That'll teach you to steal my canoe," he snarled.

Blood spurted from both my nostrils and sprayed all over
my shirt. I was furious. "Look what you did, Buster, you
got blood and mud all over my good shirt and pants."

Buster was shocked. Even a lummox like him knew that
wearing your good shirt and pants put you off limits for
beating up.

"Gee," he said, "I dint know. How come you wearing
your good shirt and pants in the middle of summer?"

"Piano lessons," I said. "I'm on my way to start taking
piano lessons from Miss Swartz."

"Geez, how could your mom do that to you?"

"Beats me," I said, brushing away at the mud on my good pants. "You know women."

"Kinda," said Buster. "Hey, guy, I dint mean to hit you in the nose. I was aiming for your eye. You musta moved."

"Yeah," I said. "It was all my fault. I hope you won't hold it against me."

"Naw, no hard feelin's. Here, let me help you with that nosebleed." Buster tore two pieces of cloth from his grungy T-shirt and, tilting my head back by my hair, stuffed them up my nostrils. "There! Now you won't drip blood all over Miss Swartz's piano."

It bothered me a little, having pieces of Buster's T-shirt so near my brain, but I thanked him, climbed back on my bike, and rode off to my lesson. I arrived at Miss Swartz's without further incident, except that Skip Holly's dog, Grover, raced out and grabbed the leg of my good pants, practically tearing it off at the knee. Already piano lessons were starting to get on my nerves, and I hadn't even had one yet. The worst, however, was still to come.

Miss Swartz was about the fussiest person I've ever known. When she opened the door to let me in, a look of undiluted horror spread across her face. Scared me. I glanced over my shoulder to make sure some wild man with an ax or something wasn't sneaking up behind me, but nobody was there. It was none other than me, her new piano pupil, Miss Swartz was staring at. She looked as if she was about to start gagging, polite, dainty gagging I'm sure, but gagging nonetheless.

Miss Swartz took me by the collar and dragged me through her fussy living room to her fussy bathroom and made me wash my face and hands and remove the pieces of

Buster's T-shirt, which had worked fine for stopping my
nosebleed. Then she spread newspapers on her piano bench
and we sat down on them to begin my first lesson. It was
awful. She made me sit up unnaturally straight and hold
my arms and hands and fingers just so. The first song I was
supposed to learn had three notes in it and was something
called "The Fairy Picnic." Well, it was a pretty sorry picnic
if you asked me, even for fairies. I came right out and told
Miss Swartz that I didn't think I was going to enjoy my
piano lessons.

"I don't think I'll enjoy them much either," she said,
"but one must do what one must do."

The minute the lesson was over she gave me a thin little
music book and ushered me out the door with orders to
practice "The Fairy Picnic" an hour a day for the next
week. Fat chance! She never even mentioned the custard.
As I was going down the walk, my nerves all frazzled and
jumpy, I noticed a man out front peering under the hood
of his car.

"Engine trouble," he explained to me. "I have to call a
mechanic. Know anyone around here with a telephone?"

"Miss Swartz here has one, but she'll make you wash
that grease off your hands before she lets you use it."

"Thanks, son. I owe you one."

"No problem, Mr. Jefferies."

I still had five or six hours of daylight left to enjoy myself.
What I needed was some quiet and solitude to calm my
nerves. What better than paddling a canoe down on the
creek? I leaped on my bike and headed home.

Zumbo and
the Misty Mountain
Ghosts

Moving with the effortless ease of the natural athlete, I ascended one of the steeper slopes of Misty Mountain. Off to my right, I could hear Jim Zumbo practicing his elk call. I knew it was Zumbo because of the distinctive sound of his call: "Here, elk! Here, elk!"

I don't know why Zumbo was practicing his elk call, because it's pretty simple to master. Also, we were hunting turkeys. I moved off in his direction and found him sitting on a log gazing off over the vast expanse of the Misty Mountain Ranch, which is about the size of Connecticut. The ranch is so big and so remote that a hundred or so years ago it had its own town—houses for the ranch hands and their families, a school, a mercantile store, a saloon, a hotel, and even its own cemetery. Now all that remained of the town was the hotel, an empty, two-story wooden structure jutting up forlornly from the prairie, and, of course, the cemetery.

Jim pointed off at the hotel. "It's getting late," he said. "By the time we work our way back down the mountain, it'll be dark. The ranch foreman says there's a couple of cots in the hotel, and we're welcome to roll our sleeping bags out on them for the night. We can get up early and drive back to town by nine in the morning. What say?"

The town Jim referred to was a hundred miles away. We had to be there at nine in the morning, because we were scheduled to participate in a panel discussion at a conference. Since we had to be in the area for the conference anyway, we had decided to squeeze in a quick turkey hunt on the Misty Mountain Ranch. (I prefer to hunt slow turkeys, but Jim insisted on quick ones.) Even from the distance, it was evident that the old hotel was still in good enough shape to give us reasonable shelter.

"Gosh, I don't know," I said. "I just have an odd feeling about the hotel, like how come the ranch owners did away with all the rest of the town and left only the hotel?"

"The way I hear it, the town got so run down and dilapidated that it became an eyesore, and the owners decided to burn it to the ground. So the ranch hands burned down all the building but the hotel. When they tried to set fire to it, something kept blowing out the matches. So they left it."

"I thought that might be the case," I said.

"Ha!" Jim laughed. "I just made that up. You're so gullible, McManus. You aren't afraid of ghosts, are you?"

"Me? Afraid of ghosts? Of course not!" Although I am not overly fond of ghosts, I am certainly not afraid of them. I am not even sure they exist. On the other hand, I'm not sure they don't exist. Over the years I have had several encounters with phenomena that might be ghosts, but urgent business elsewhere required that I depart the premises in haste, and I was therefore unable to conduct a proper scientific investigation, much to my disappointment.

I was once relaxing in my office at home when an empty pair of chest waders came clumping through the door. Simultaneously, I noticed that I had levitated several inches off my chair and the book I had been reading left my hands and ricocheted off several walls and the ceiling. Time seemed to stand still, something I had no intention of doing myself, as soon as gravity canceled out my levitation, and I could gain sufficient traction. Then a voice from the waders said, "Look at me, Grandpa." I immediately investigated the waders and found a small, redheaded child concealed inside. Mimicking the child's favorite television-show host, I asked if he could say "cardiac arrest." He couldn't, although that evening at dinner he spoke, with great clarity, several other words he had learned that day. Despite the boy's refusal to reveal the source of his new words, because it was a secret between him and his grandpa, the usual suspect was apprehended and sentenced to the "silent treatment" and stern looks until well after dessert.

Then there was the time Uncle Shamus, dead for ten years, showed up in my garage and asked for the return of a fly rod he had apparently loaned me. As I stood there calmly sucking garage-floor debris into my lungs, I vaguely wondered what use a dead man had for a fly rod and whether it was worth pursuing the subject with a ghost. But the apparition turned out to be none other than my live neighbor Al Finley, who in silhouette and tone of voice bears a striking resemblance to poor Shamus, so much so in fact that I almost panicked and returned the fly rod.

Thus are so-called supernatural phenomena easily explained away as nothing more than misapprehended effects of commonplace causes, and, of course, the occasional ghost.

In any case, I was not about to engage in a discussion of parapsychology with Zumbo, whose reasoning processes have been profoundly distorted by an education in the sciences. As a result, we were soon hauling our sleeping bags from our car to the hotel, which stared hungrily down at us with its empty window sockets. The moon was up, with the traditional shreds of cloud scudding across it. A breeze stirred the prairie grass and sent tumbleweeds bounding about like frantic skeletons of giant insects, giving me the distinct feeling I was about to step inside a Stephen King novel.

In short order, however, we had our propane lantern burning brightly in the hotel kitchen and our supper sizzling away on our propane camp stove. A couple of the ranch hands, Jeb and Biff, came in and joined us for supper and a little bourbon sipping afterward. We exchanged a few hunting and fishing tales and then drifted into ghost stories, for which the eerie setting was most appropriate, even to excess. It wasn't long before we were glancing over our shoulders and smoothing down the hairs on the backs of our necks. The stories soon eroded even Zumbo's education in the sciences, particularly when the lantern began to fade from lack of fuel. As darkness settled over the kitchen, Jeb and Biff arose from the table in unison and departed the premises with an urgency neither bothered to explain, which was probably just as well.

"Don't go!" I shouted after them. "Wait! We have more bourbon!"

"Come back!" Jim shouted. "Spend the night!"

But Jeb and Biff sped away into the darkness, leaving behind only faint aromas of burnt rubber and foul exhaust, which struck me as odd, since they weren't driving a vehicle.

"Well," Jim said, "we might as well turn in. But remember, we have to get up early. We've got to be at that conference no later than nine, and it's a good two-hour drive."

"True," I said. "So what would you think about starting for town right now?"

"No way," Jim said. "I'm too tired. Grab your sleeping bag. We each have a reserved room at the top of the stairs."

"Why don't we both sleep in the same room?" I suggested.

"Not a chance," Jim said. "Your snoring keeps me awake."

At the top of the stairs, Zumbo and I had a brief scuffle to see who got to take our lone flashlight. As usual, he won. I walked into my room and slammed the door. A shaft of moonlight revealed an old army cot next to the window. I rolled out my sleeping bag on the cot, and then sat down on it to enjoy the moonlit landscape, the low, rolling prairie hills and tall grass undulating in the wind like silvery ocean waves. It was all quite nice. I stripped to my shorts, slipped into my mummy bag, and, sedated by bourbon and merciful exhaustion, soon was fast asleep, despite some minor lingering effects from the session of ghost stories, not least of which were goose bumps of a size that produced the sensation of sleeping on a bed of marbles. My intention was to snooze so deeply and soundly as to be totally oblivious to all creaks, cracks, moans, and bumps in the night.

Sometime past midnight, however, I began to dream that

I was still looking out my hotel room window at the peaceful, moonlit landscape. The scene in my dream was exactly
as I had viewed it before going to sleep. So far so good.
But as I sat there enjoying the dream scene, I detected some
movement among the swaying grasses a couple hundred
yards away, in the direction of the old town's cemetery.
Walking slowly toward the town came a tall human figure,
a man. He was soon joined by another man. My dream self
wondered if the two were perhaps Jeb and Biff, sneaking
back to execute some practical joke on Jim and me.

Then the two figures were joined by a dozen other figures, both men and women and even some children. Soon
there was a whole skirmish line of them, advancing toward
the hotel. "What's going on here?" my dream self asked.
"Who are these people? What do they want?" As the dream
people moved closer to the former outskirts of town, I noticed that they were all dressed in old-fashioned clothes—
clothes you might expect ranch people of the last century to
wear!

"Jeepers criminy!" my dream self exclaimed. "These are
the townspeople of a hundred years ago returning to their
lost town!" (It is likely that my real self actually blurted out
the "Jeepers criminy" part of the above exclamation, because at that moment something awakened Zumbo in the
next room.) My dream self stared with increasing intensity
out the window at the approaching townspeople, all of whom
appeared pleasant and attractive, and even quite healthy, except
for the minor detail that *I could see right through them!*

The townspeople strode purposefully into the nonexistent
town, while both my dream self and real self sweated copi-
ously. Then it occurred to me what the townspeople of a
hundred years ago were doing. They were returning to their

homes! But their homes were gone! What would they do when they discovered their homes were gone? Why, they would come to the hotel! They would be angry! They would want to know what Jim and I had done with their houses! And they probably wouldn't be satisfied with our explanations.

Zumbo, drowsily awake in the other room, picked up his watch. Because he was holding the watch upside down, he read the time as 7:00 rather than the actual time, 1:30. "Yowp!" he cried, snapping wide awake. "We'll be late for the conference!"

Thinking I'd heard an agonized shout, I popped upright on my cot. I looked out the window. Everything was just the same as in my dream, except the townspeople were gone. *Why sure,* I thought, *they've moved out of the range of my vision and are looking for their houses! They're probably headed for the hotel right now! They might be coming through the door this instant! Probably their shouting I'd heard!*

The door to my room banged open with such force it almost flew off its hinges. Since I expected none other than an angry mob of long-dead townspeople, ghostly lynch rope in hand, my eyeballs strained at their tethers while havoc played chopsticks with my bodily functions. But it was Zumbo who lunged in, wearing only his shorts. His voice was panicky. "Get up! Get up!" he screamed at me. "We're got to get out of here! Fast!"

Naturally, having forgotten all about the conference, I assumed that Jim, too, had witnessed the approach of the townspeople. Besides that, I had been staring out the window and knew it was still the middle of the night. The only explanation for Jim's panic was that he, too, had seen the ghosts approaching.

Zumbo seemed shocked by the immediacy and explosive energy of my response. According to his later report, I did two laps around the walls of the room at shoulder height to pick up sufficient momentum for my exit from the premises. He was exaggerating, of course. I doubt I was ever more than three feet off the floor even at peak acceleration. Nor did I ever see any evidence that pieces of my sleeping bag zipper were imbedded in the walls.

Jim, of course, was somewhat confused, never before having seen me display such concern over being late for a conference or anything else for that matter. I for my part wondered why Jim just stood there in his shorts with his mouth agape during an emergency of such potentially dreadful consequences, like our being dragged off into the previous century by a bunch of irate people you could see through.

Recovering from his stupor, Jim consulted his watch again and now read the time correctly.

"Wait!" he yelled. "I made a mistake. It's only one-thirty in the morning, not seven o'clock! Ha ha! I guess the joke's on me. Go back to sleep."

Easy for Jim to say.

The Road Hunter

While I was tidying up the garage the other day, my wife, Bun, came out to critique my efforts.

"Why don't you throw some of this junk away?" she critiqued. "Somebody's going to get caught in a cave-in someday."

"Don't exaggerate," I said, adjusting the miner's light on my helmet. "As soon as I finish putting some more timbers in Tunnel Three, it will be perfectly safe."

Bun kicked at a little green metal box near an air shaft. "What's this?"

"Some keepsakes," I said. "I have a lot of fond memories in that little box."

"Oh, yeah?" she said, bending over and unsnapping the lid. "What kind of fond memories?"

"Uh, you know, hunting and fishing trips I particularly enjoyed. That sort of thing."

Bun extracted from the box a lock of curly blond hair tied with a ribbon. "What were you hunting on this trip?" Her eyes had narrowed to such hard little slits it was difficult to detect the bemused twinkle in them.

For a feverish moment the fond memory associated with the lock of hair eluded my attempt at recall. Then it all came back to me, the recollection so sharp and clear it raised beads of sweat on my brow.

"That's some of Buck's hair," I explained.

"Buck's as bald as a grapefruit."

"Yeah," I said. "And about as smart. But back when this fond memory originated, Buck had beautiful curly blond hair. It was his pride and joy, his crowning glory. He couldn't pass a reflective surface of any kind without stopping to admire his golden locks and caress them with his ever-present comb. Buck's comb was practically an anatomical appendage. He was fascinated by his own hair. It was as if he carried his hobby around on top of his head. And now all that's left of his hair is a ragged little tuft in a tin box on the floor of a garage. Sad to say, that box contains some bits and pieces of what I once was, too."

"No kidding," Bun said. "Well, I'm sure not sticking my fingers in there again. So what's the fond memory associated with this lock of Buck's hair?"

I'm five years younger than Cousin Buck, which isn't much now, but back when I was thirteen and Buck was eighteen, it was a lot. I didn't have a father or a big brother to take me hunting and fishing and teach me things, so I often had to make do with Buck. Buck's intellect peaked at about age eighteen, and for several years he knew just about everything worth knowing. He confided this to me himself, so I'm sure it's true. Alas, his intellect began to fade a few years later, and it wasn't long before you could strike it with a simple idea and not get so much as a spark, let alone illumination. For several years, though, Buck and I made a great team. He knew everything and I knew nothing. We balanced each other out.

If Buck stopped by while I was making a slingshot, he'd say, "That ain't no way to make a slingshot." Then he would tell me how to make a slingshot. If I bought a new fishing fly to replace my old one, Buck would say, "That fly ain't no good. You should've bought . . ." If I was digging worms for fish bait, Buck would say, "That ain't no way to dig worms. How you dig worms is . . ." And so on. I guess I was too dumb to fully appreciate Buck's enormous intellect during the time that it flourished. Mostly, it just got on my nerves. For several wonderful years, though, Buck was my hero.

It was during this period that Buck briefly became a road hunter. I cannot even begin to tell how humiliated I was to learn that my hero, indeed, one of my own relatives, had sunk so low as to hunt from the seat of a car. In the time and place of my youth, there were few people more despised than a road hunter. A conversation in the barber shop, for example, might go something like this:

"Hear Blacky got drunk t'other night, wrecked the saloon and put nine people in the hospital."

"Um."

"I suppose he was still mad about gettin' arrested for stealin' hogs."

"Um."

"Tricked Widow Belfrey into sellin' him her car and ain't

paid her a cent for it. Poor old woman has to walk fifteen
miles to town and pull her groceries home in a little red
wagon.''

"Um.''

"Blacky's a road hunter, too, ya know.''

"A road hunter! Why that dirty no good rotten scum . . . !''

Everybody understood that road-hunting was one of the
most contemptible of all human activities. Parents might
have a son grow up to become a deacon in the church, a
medical doctor, a faithful husband, a loving father, and a
Republican. But if that son also turned out to be a road
hunter, they would know they had failed miserably in his
upbringing. That is why I was so ashamed when I began to
suspect that Buck had become a road hunter. I was afraid,
too, because I knew that God would punish him severely
for sinking into such a slothful state that he would actually
hunt deer from the seat of his car. And that is exactly what
happened.

Only a week remained in hunting season, and Buck
hadn't got his deer yet. He stopped by my house one day a
little before noon and told me it was time he taught me
something about deer hunting. Even though my mother
considered me too young to hunt deer myself, I had studied
deer hunting in *Outdoor Life* for many years and knew how
it was supposed to be done. Already I sensed something
peculiar about this proposed hunt.

"It's almost noon,'' I said. "Deer hunts start at four in
the morning. You got to be out in the woods by the crack
of dawn.''

"Crack of dawn my elbow,'' Buck said. "You goin' or
not?''

Of course I was going. I didn't get invited along on that

many deer hunts that I could afford to turn any down. Still, there was something strange about this hunt, something that made me vaguely uneasy. There was Buck's car, of course. That would make anyone uneasy. Its upholstery looked as if it had served as furnishings for a puppy kennel. All the fabric had been ripped off the interior of the roof, exposing a web of what looked like chicken wire attached to metal crossbars, one of which was directly over the front seat, apparently functioning as a hard object on which to bang your head. The floorboards had rusted out, providing a nice view of the road surface rushing by between your feet. I could scarcely wait until I was old enough to own a hunting vehicle just like it.

We drove up into the Twenty Mile Creek drainage and turned off onto a logging road. After a bit, we passed old Sam Smith's cabin. Buck kept driving and driving and driving, circling around one mountain and then another. I became so confused with all the driving that I didn't have the slightest notion where we were. Then we passed old Sam Smith's cabin. I thought about this for a while. "Where you plan on hunting, Buck?" I asked.

"I'm still looking for just the right place."

"Well, I think we should get out and hike up onto that ridge above Ruby Lake. That's a good place for mulies."

"No, it ain't," Buck said. "It ain't no good for mulies. Anyway, I'll let you know when I find the right place for us to hunt."

We drove another twenty miles or so. I was getting so bored I could hardly stand it. Then we passed a little log cabin.

"Hey," I said. "Isn't that . . . ?"

"Sam Smith's cabin," Buck said. "Why do you ask?"

"Buck," I said, "I know what you're doing. You're not fooling me one bit. You're road-hunting!"

"Am not," Buck said, yawning. "Now listen careful. I'm only going to explain this to you once. Road-hunting is where you go out and drive around on roads looking for a game animal to shoot. But if you're driving around looking for a place to hunt, to actually get out and look for signs and rattle some antlers and all that, and you happen to spot a deer on a sidehill near the road and you shoot it, well that's not road-hunting but regular hunting, which is what I'm engaged in here. You see? Now shut up."

It still seemed like road-hunting to me, but I shut up. We drove around for another hour looking for a place to hunt, passing Sam Smith's cabin a couple more times, and by then it was too dark to shoot.

"We shouldn't have wasted all this time with your road-hunting," I said to Buck. "If we had got out and done some real hunting, we'd have a deer by now."

"Shut up about road-hunting," Buck snarled. "I told you we was just looking for a place to hunt."

I could tell from his tone that he felt guilty, that he knew he had been road-hunting all along. I had seen how he would sneak up over the top of a hill in low gear, hoping to surprise a buck on the other side. A road hunter's idea of stealth is to roll down a car window quietly. He thinks "going on a stand" is to sit in his car near a clear-cut with the radio and heater on, sipping hot coffee, eating a sandwich, and reading a comic book. That was what my hero had become, the epitome of slothfulness, a road hunter.

We were now headed back down the steep part of Twenty Mile Creek Road. Buck, as was his practice to save gas, had shifted to neutral, turned off the ignition, and was coasting. We kept picking up speed.

"Better slow down, Buck," I said nervously. "We're nearly to Good Gosh Almighty Curve."

"I know what I'm doing," Buck said. "If you'd just pay attention, I could teach you something about mountain driving. See, what I'm doing here is using gravity to save on fuel consumption and—"

We hit a tremendous bump. Buck and I bounced clear up to the ceiling and banged our heads on the crossbar that had been put there for that purpose. I crashed back down on the seat and, still dazed, glanced over to see if Buck was all right. He hadn't come down yet! I blinked my eyes and rubbed my head. Buck was still suspended in the air!

"Stop fooling around, Buck!" I yelled. "We're going too darn fast!"

Then I saw what had happened. Buck's hair had caught between the roof and the crossbar. He was hanging by his hair! His thrashing feet couldn't reach the brake! His clawing fingers couldn't reach the steering wheel! We were racing down the mountain totally out of control.

"The brake! The brake!" Buck screeched from up above. "Hit the brake!"

I started jamming my foot in the general direction of the brake pedal, but without success. Then I scrambled down under the dash and Buck's flailing legs and tried to push the brake with my hand. I knew Good Gosh Almighty Curve was zooming up at us. I suddenly realized what was happening: God was punishing Buck for road-hunting! I started to pray: "Lord, kill Buck if you must for road-hunting, but let me go. I was just along for the ride!"

Then we were into the curve. Miraculously, we sailed around it on two wheels, sending a shower of gravel out into dark space. The car dropped onto all fours and rocketed down the straight stretch true as an arrow. God had answered my prayer. He had given Buck the good sense to steer around the curve with his feet. It was the first and only time I ever saw two sets of toes clamped onto a steering wheel, despite the impediment of boot soles.

A second later, we hit another big bump, which jerked Buck loose from the bar and dropped him back down on the seat. He hit the brake and the car slid to a stop. Buck eventually admitted the ordeal took a lot out of him. I suppose he meant the sizable tuft of hair, which I later retrieved from the bar on the roof and saved as a memento of the occasion. We both sat there sweating and shaking in the stillness of the night. Buck had a terrible expression on his face. I know the expression on my face was almost as bad, because I checked it the next morning in a mirror.

"Let this be a lesson to you, Buck," I croaked. "God hates road hunters!"

He stared silently at me for a moment, his trembling lips struggling to form the right words, words that would express his true feelings for me in that moment of our shared terror and narrow escape, words that defined the ties that bound us together even beyond those of blood. "Do me a favor," he said. "Shut your yap!"

Five years later, Buck was bald as a grapefruit. God had let him live, but took the first tuft of hair as a down payment for the sin of road-hunting and collected the rest in installments.

Why Is It?

Why is it whenever a tackle box slips out of your hand it never falls right side up and closed?

Why is it the hunting partner who is going to rendezvous with you at the old apple orchard at noon never does?

Why is it even though you own four thousand dollars' worth of fine tools you end up repairing an expensive piece of sporting equipment with a flat rock and a wooden match?

Why is it shortly before she drifts blissfully off to sleep on the first night of a tent-camping trip, your wife's last words are: "What's that? Did you hear that strange noise outside the tent just now?"

Why is it your kid thinks it so funny to test the clicker on his reel while you are walking through tall grass in rattle-snake country?

Why is it your air mattress springs a leak on the first night of a five-night backpacking trip and not when your kid was using it as a trampoline on the driveway?

Why is it a woman who catches more fish than you thinks that's such an interesting topic of conversation at parties?

Why is it the person who is supposed to net the largest fish you have ever hooked in your life suddenly loses his depth perception, all physical coordination, any sense of urgency, and, quite often, the net?

Why is it when the world's largest bass snaps your line right at the boat your fishing companion is your priest, minister, rabbi, or, worst of all, your little grandson, who later asks his mother, "Mommy, what kind of fish is a bleeping bleep bleep bleep bass?"

Why is it your hunting partner's car always develops a funny sound in the transmission when it's his turn to provide the hunting vehicle?

Why is it fish and deer can't keep the same hours as humans?

Why is it you reach your peak physical condition the last day of elk season and not the first?

Why is it the older you get the more you begin to feel that actually shooting something on a hunting trip is rather a nuisance?

Why is it you are always alone when you make the greatest shot of your life, and your great misses are always made in front of a crowd of sadistic hecklers?

Why is it game birds can sense that you have just changed the choke setting on your shotgun?

Why is it the day's only flock of ducks comes in while you are putting out your decoys?

Why is it when a storm confines you to a small tent for two days your companion is never an attractive person of the opposite sex but an unattractive person of the same sex who passes the time by trying to perfect his John Wayne impersonation?

Why is it illegal to shoot a person who practices his John Wayne impersonation for two full days in a small tent?

Why is it a fly will zip inside the ear of the person who is spreading the barbed wires of a fence for you to crawl through?

Why is it outdoorsmen don't leave the key to their vehicle in the ignition rather than hiding it on top of the left rear tire?

Why is it you develop a mysterious but temporary pain in your chest two days before you are supposed to take the Cub Scouts on their first all-nighter?

Why is it all rope is always six inches too short rather than six inches too long?

Why is it trailer lights work only during the daytime?

Why is it boat manufacturers have never built a boat the right size?

Why is it wives cannot see the necessity of owning twenty-seven guns, most of which you never shoot?

Why is it the person who tells you to "take a running jump, you can make it to the other side" turns out to be a person with notoriously bad depth perception or a rotten sense of humor?

Why is it you can't replace the starter cord on your outboard motor without that big spring leaping out and grabbing you by the throat?

Why is it that the Forest Service has insisted upon making the trails so much steeper and longer over the past ten years?

Why is it most of the gear in a backpack eventually ends up in your pockets?

Why is it pamphlets of hunting and fishing regulations have become only slightly less complicated than a treatise on nuclear fusion?

Why is it psychiatrists think nervous breakdowns in mothers may be attributed to small boys carrying spare fishing works in their shirt pockets?

Why is it after you have hiked five miles in to a campsite on public land you find that nine thousand cows recently camped there?

Why is it cows camped on public land aren't considered public cows, or as we hunters like to say, slow elk?

Why is it your child gets that peculiar look on his face when you ask for your two-hundred-dollar binoculars you loaned him three miles back on the trail?

Why is it outdoorsmen who played with black powder during their youth have only scar tissue for eyebrows?

Why is it the first you hear of your partner's back problems (hypertension, irregular heartbeat, bad knee, etc.) is shortly after you've shot an elk at the bottom of a steep canyon?

Why is it as soon as you buy the ultimate electronic fish-finder the really ultimate fish-finder is put on the market?

Why is it outdoorsmen don't realize they can't live without a piece of gear until they first see it in a catalog?

Why is it new inventions that will transform fishing never transform fishing?

Why is it fish-finders can find fish but can't make them bite?

Why is it wives can never understand why an outdoorsman needs twenty-three different kinds of boots and shoes?

Why is it no one ever invented a compass that points in a useful direction—toward the place where you parked your car, for example?

Why is it on television fishing shows the anglers never get skunked?

Why is it when you need to tie a nail knot you never have a nail?

Why is it you never think to ask an outfitter why your horse is named Jitterbug until you are riding it along a thousand-foot drop-off?

Why is it white-water rafting guides think it's so funny to yell, "Quick, everybody paddle back upstream!"

Why is it bush pilots think it helps on takeoff from small lakes to say, "Sit light on your seats, boys, and I think we can clear that ridge."

Why is it that at wild-game dinners someone always bursts into gleeful laughter and cries, "I bet you don't know what that was you just ate!"

Why is it wives can't just accept the biological mystery of guns reproducing in gun cabinets, and let it go at that?

Why is it when your fishing partner catches fish it's a matter of skill and when you catch fish it's a matter of luck?

Why is it wives can't just accept the mystery of an outdoorsman's needing a minimum of five boats, and let it go at that?

Why is it wives can't just accept the mystery of why an outdoorsman absolutely needs so much stuff, and let it go at that?

Why is it after you have packed a six-pack of beverage in over a hot and dusty trail and stored it in an icy stream to cool, you return to find only a note that says, "Thank you, Lord!"

The Late Great Fourth

These days the Fourth of July seems more whimper than bang. I can remember a time when the Fourth wasn't a day but a season, a progressive explosion starting in June, peaking on July fourth, and fading out near August. Most guys didn't even recover from their injuries until Halloween. Eyebrows finished growing back in about Christmas. Some of them never did. It was as though we had been born with a secret message recorded in our genes: "On the Fourth of July after the age of five your mission is to self-destruct."

The big excitement on the Fourth nowadays is when my grandchildren go out in the backyard and embroider the night with a few sparklers. The only loud noise is my wife's yelling: "Not so close to your face! Don't let the sparks fall on your clothes! Watch out!"

Why, heck. Nobody did that much yelling when I was a

kid unless a fragment of flaming magnesium burned through somebody's hide. Even then it wasn't a mother doing the yelling. After the Fourth, most parents were accustomed to their children looking like cinders. When Mom reported to old Dad that little Harold had been caught smoking again, she didn't mean cigarettes.

There's not a kid in our whole neighborhood now who knows the simple delight of having a firecracker go off in his fingers before he can throw it. And it's probably a good thing: the average kid nowadays doesn't know how to react properly after such an event—thrusting the fingers into the mouth, pulling them out again to make sure they're still attached, then tucking them in the crotch and doing a triple-time crouch-hop around the yard, all the time trying to think of a joke to crack so the guys will know he's no sissy.

Occasionally, I'll meet a man whose thumb and forefinger are shaped like matching shoehorns, and I'll know that here is a veteran of ancient Fourths, a person who as a youngster learned too late he didn't possess quick enough hands for throwing firecrackers.

"The Fourth sure isn't what it used to be, is it?" I'll say, in hope of striking up a conversation.

"What's that?" he'll reply, blinking bald eyes and cocking his shoehorns behind a cauliflower ear. "Speak up, man!"

Even the Fourth of July parades of today are but crepe-paper ghosts of their former selves. The floats never seem to break down. In the olden days, along with the hilarious shovel-wielding routines of the clowns who followed the Sheriff's Posse, conked-out floats provided much of the comedy. Even now I remember what great fun it was watching fourteen Elks push their nine-thousand-pound float the last

mile of the parade. Men cheered and women wept when the
float powered by fourteen straining Elks crept up the Pine
Street hill to the finish line. I once heard a logger among
the spectators comment that maybe the clowns should follow
the Elk float, but the clowns weren't needed: the Elk float
was funny enough just as it was. In fact, it was wonderful.
I wouldn't be surprised if the Elks didn't *intend* for their float
to break down, just for the laughs.

Then there was the Fourth of July carnival, the most
exciting event of the year. And dangerous, too. But we
weren't a bunch of rubes. We knew carnival people were
evil, possibly even criminals on the lam, and that the carnival always attracted pickpockets and wicked women. My
pocket went unpicked, but probably only because I kept
my hand in it, clutching my sweaty dimes and quarters.
But once, when I was about fifteen, I did have a brief
affair with a wicked carnival woman. My pulse still quick-
ens at the memory.

Her lips were scarlet, her eyelids blue, and her hair the
color of sunset. As I sauntered past her concession booth,
she caught my eye and beckoned me over with a sultry
smile and a toss of her sunset head. I gave her a knowing
grin, which I had perfected for just such an occasion, and
started to move on, casually dismissing the sharp pangs
of panic that started in my midsection and spread to
extremities. Then she gave me a long, languorous wink
that temporarily arrested several of my vital functions.
Well shoot, I said to myself, it might be fun to toy with
her emotions a bit, since she seems so enamored of me. I
sauntered over and bought a set of darts to throw at her
balloon board.

Immediately after I had blown my last dime on the

darts, she suddenly realized that I had merely been dallying with her. She broke off our relationship on the spot, and turned her attention to a gullible kid passing by, her wink stopping him like an ice pick through the heart. I laughed throatily, tossed my jacket over my shoulder, and sauntered off, secure in the knowledge that I had also perfected my sauntering.

Much older and wiser now, I'm fairly certain that the goal of the carnival people was to extract every last cent from every last simple soul to fall under their spell. There were even little machines designed like drag lines, with which, for a penny, you could attempt to grab a wonderful prize with the jaws at the end of the line. I blew nearly a buck trying to fish out a beautiful silver-and-gold harmonica and ended up with a crummy paper mustache. Somehow, the jaws never seemed quite strong enough to grasp the harmonica. You'd think the carnival people would have realized that and corrected it.

One of my worst experiences at a Fourth of July carnival resulted from bumping into my former girlfriend, Olga Bonemarrow. Olga had recently terminated our romance in the bud, claiming I didn't know how to treat girls with proper respect. That was ridiculous. She simply wasn't accustomed to my suave and debonair manners.

"Hey, Bonemarrow," I said. "How about riding the Octopus with me?"

"Naw," she replied. "The Octopus makes me throw up."

"It doesn't either," I said. "Nothing makes you throw up."

"It does, too. Sometimes you make me throw up."

"I'll pay for your ride."

"Okay. But the Octopus still makes me throw up."

"Yeah, right."

The Octopus really did make Olga throw up. What we called the Octopus had eight long steel arms that spun around and swooped up and down. On the end of each arm was a wire basket to hold the riders so they couldn't fall out or escape. At certain points during the swooping and whirling, the basket would spin madly. After the first of these spins, Olga said, "I'm going to be sick!"

I stared in swirling horror as her rosy complexion changed first to chalk white and then to a pale but ominous green. So there I was, trapped in a spinning basket fifty feet in the air with a person about to throw up! I yelled at the Octopus operator. "Stop the Octopus! Stop! There's a person here about to be sick!" The operator, obviously a criminal on the lam, responded with an evil laugh and threw the machine into high gear. Taking one quick last look at Olga's green ballooning cheeks and bulging eyes, I hurled myself to the floor of the basket. But for the lucky combination of a weak stomach, moderately good reflexes, and a working knowledge of centrifugal force, I'd have been a goner. At every violent spin of the basket, Olga threw up. Crouched on the floor and peering out like a caged animal through the wire mesh, I could see people on the ground fleeing madly away from the Octopus in all directions, attempting to escape the carnival version of acid rain. Once out of Olga's range, they turned and tried to make out the identity of the persons in the offending basket. It was embarrassing. Besides feeling faintly green myself, I particularly dreaded being recognized when Olga and I emerged from the cage after the ride. So long, suave and debonair!

"I told you the Octopus makes me sick," Olga said afterward.

I attempted to comfort her. "Boy, that's an understatement if I ever heard one!"

"I feel better now, though. In fact, I think you should buy us each a hot dog."

"I'll buy you one," I said. "As for myself, I've kind of lost my appetite—*like for about nine years!*"

"In that case, I guess I'll forgive you," she said. "But only if you take off that stupid paper mustache!"

When we were twelve years old, Peewee Thompson, Retch Sweeney, and I didn't waste any money on the Octopus, the Sword Swallower, or the Tattooed Man. We did treat ourselves to a couple of hot dogs each, for the sake of tradition, but then headed right for the tent featuring the beautiful wicked lady who purportedly danced around on a stage with all her clothes off. If there was anything we felt a compelling need to see at that time in our lives, it was a beautiful dancing woman with all her clothes off. We didn't even care if she danced. She could just stand there and chew gum, as long as she did it with her clothes off.

Nowadays seeing a naked lady is no big deal to any kid old enough to toddle past a newsstand, but back then it was like a glimpse of the other side of the moon. To us, female anatomy was just a rumor we hoped was true. And now was our chance to find out!

Alas, the barker at the tent said absolutely no children allowed. Adults only. Guards were posted at all corners of the tent, he said, to prevent youngsters from sneaking in and getting their brains petrified by the sights inside. We decided to try our luck anyway.

"How much?" we asked the ticket seller.

"Two bits," she said. "The line forms at the right, men."

Inside the tent, we squeezed into bleachers with the other

men. The tent lights dimmed, music honked from the loud-speakers, and the ratty stage curtain rattled open. The crowd tensed, twittered, tested its leers.

But what was that? The lady had danced onto the stage all right, but she wasn't naked! She was wearing about ten layers of clothes! Our bewildered eyeballs settled back into their sockets, and we blinked for the first time in five min-utes. In sullen silence, we watched the lady twist and twirl about the stage, not that easy for someone dressed like an Arctic explorer. Suddenly, with a flick of her finger, the outside layer floated to the floor. So that was it. She would *take off* the clothes. This might be worth a quarter after all. Then the lady stopped dancing, the tent lights came up, and the barker and several of his henchmen worked their way through the audience collecting quarters for the "second act."

To us: "You men gotcher quarters?"

You bet!

By the eighth act, the farmers and loggers around us were shouting, stomping, and trying to whistle through dry lips. Only about two layers of clothes, three at the most, to go.

I extended a sweaty palm. "Loan me a quarter for the next act, Peewee."

Peewee's voice squeaked with panic: "I was gonna ask you for one!"

"I ain't got none neither!" Retch croaked.

The barker loomed in front of us. "Let's have them quar-ters, men."

Wrenching our eyes away from the stage, we tried to plead with him, to beg, if he had even a shred of decency he would let us . . . !

"Hey, what you kids doing in here, anyway? This ain't

no kinda show for kids! Wanna git yer brains petrified?
Clear out! Now!''

We shuffled glumly out of the tent, flat broke, without so
much as a dime left for cotton candy. The veil had almost
lifted for us on the wondrous mystery of female anatomy,
but then had slammed back down with a steely thud. For
three measly quarters more, we would have known the naked truth!

"Whose idea was it we buy them hot dogs?" Retch
growled. "Our one chance to see a naked lady, and we blow
it on some lousy hot dogs!"

Every Fourth of July, Uncle Finn would show up at our
farm with eight or ten boxes crammed with a delicious variety of high-explosive fireworks. One thing about Uncle
Finn, he knew how to celebrate the Fourth.

"How can he afford all those expensive fireworks?" my
mother asked one memorable Fourth. "Maybe he's given
up drinking."

"It's possible," my stepfather, Hank, replied. "I read
just the other day hell had frozen over."

Several dozen of our relatives and friends showed up to
watch Uncle Finn's fireworks. A gargantuan picnic supper was spread on tables and blankets across our lawn,
and everybody sat there and ate and watched Finn ignite
his arsenal on the driveway, the rockets arcing up and
bursting into fiery blossoms over the hayfield. Part of my
uncle's showmanship consisted of assuming an air of great
gravity as he lit each fuse and then dashed madly back
behind the picnickers, partly out of caution, but mostly
to savor better the cries of "Oooooooo! Look at that one!"
This maneuver also gave him the opportunity to sneak
another quick swig from his hip flask. Uncle Finn's degree

of intoxication thus paralleled the increasing size of the rockets. As my stepfather observed, watching the alcohol-breathed Finn wildly stab a glowing punk at a rocket fuse, one never knew which was going to be shot off—the rocket, Finn, or both.

At the culmination of the fireworks extravaganza, Uncle Finn staggered forth with a rocket that looked as if it could bring down a B-29. It was a squat, ugly green projectile, armed with multiple warheads, three in all, each only slightly smaller than a tennis ball. "Oh my!" spectators cried. "Good heavens!" Uncle Finn proudly placed the monster on the old picnic table he used for a launching pad. In his usual fashion at this stage of the game, he grappled with the rocket for several breathless seconds in his efforts to get the glowing punk in contact with the fuse. At last succeeding, he turned, bowed to the applauding spectators, and said "Tuh-TAAHHHHH!" Then he tripped and fell flat, accidentally kicking the leg of the picnic table. The rocket toppled over, its warheads covering the startled picnickers like the guns of the James gang! A second later, the rocket went off with a *POW!* and a *WHOOSH!* The screaming warheads streaked over the prostrate Finn and exploded in rapid sequence at ground zero: *BANG!BANG!BANG!*

In ringing silence, the clouds of smoke slowly rose and drifted away, revealing a desolate scene: potato salad strewn about, smoldering rocket confetti fluttering into the remains of strawberry shortcake, half-eaten pieces of fried chicken scattered hither and yon. Fortunately, no one was injured. This was due to the prompt and orderly fashion with which the yard had been evacuated. The orderliness, perhaps, did not amount to all that much, and probably should be dismissed as inconsequential. It is the amazing *promptness* that mostly stands out in my memory. I am still moved by the image of so many family friends and relatives rising as a single unit and flying for cover like a glob of humanity fired from a giant slingshot, pre-stretched and hung on a hair trigger. Although the immediate impression was one of togetherness, participants in the event later recalled the spirit of the moment as being that of every man, woman, and child for himself. Old Jake Saunders, who earlier had tottered into the yard on the arm of his grandson, was so inspired by the sight of the warheads trained on him that he fought his way out of the pack and took the lead, setting a brisk pace for the rest of us, and even managed to clear the picket fence at the far side of the yard by several inches. The fence wasn't particularly high, but it made a fair jump for a man both old and lame and with a ham sandwich still in his mouth. Just before the rocket went off, Hank said, he glanced back to check on my grandmother, more out of curiosity than anything else, but the yard was already empty, except for several glasses of lemonade suspended in the air. He said that even though Gram trailed the pack, she ''was burning rubber'' when her wheelchair shot past him. But Gram said to pay Hank no mind; he was just exaggerating again.

The next Fourth of July, Uncle Finn was forced to set off his fireworks display a hundred yards out in the hay field. Even then the spectators didn't feel entirely safe, but, as old Saunders pointed out, they would have a little more time to get traction.

Those late, great Fourths are gone forever, leaving me only with the memories, not to mention a dozen scars, bald eyes, and a slight numbness in my fingers from discovering too late I didn't possess the reflexes for the throwing of fire-crackers. It's probably just as well. I even yelled at my grandchildren last Fourth of July: "Be careful with those sparklers! Don't hold them so close to your face! Watch out! You want to look like a cinder?" It seemed the least I could do, to stir up a little excitement.

Camping In

When it comes to camping out nowadays, my wife, Bun, prefers camping in She says she likes a little something extra between her and the hard, cold ground, preferably several floors of a luxury hotel.

I must admit that I myself do most of my camping in my old pickup camper. It's adequate for Bun and me, and a darn sight cheaper than a luxury hotel. My camper may not be a luxury hotel, but it keeps Bun off the hard, cold ground and, more important, out of the boutiques. As I explain to Bun, they just don't build luxury hotels where I want to go. If they did, I probably wouldn't want to go there.

My camper is a bit small. I can almost cook breakfast without getting out of bed. "Room service again," I tell Bun. "What more could you ask for?" I keep forgetting that is a poor question to ask someone who has spent the night sleeping over the cab of a truck.

The camper is "self-contained," with its own tiny bathroom. It's a bit cramped though. Besides cooking breakfast, you can practically shave and shower without getting out of bed.

Just because a person prefers a camper and doesn't do a lot of hiking into the high country anymore, Bun interprets that as a sign of getting old and soft. The other day I heard her tell one of our grown daughters, "The curmudgeon is starting to slow down. I haven't heard him and Vern even mention hiking into Pyramid Lake this year." They both sat there chuckling over their coffee cups.

Well, first of all, I don't know why Bun would speak unkindly of my neighbor Al Finley, the curmudgeon. Al has never hiked anywhere in his life. He hates hiking. Besides, he doesn't even know my old camping buddy, Vern. If by chance Bun was suggesting that I am slowing down, I can only respond, "Nonsense!"

Just last summer, for example, Vern and I hiked into an alpine lake and camped out amid lingering drifts of snow. We had a nice time, too. The night was quiet and peaceful, at least until about eleven, when some anguished screeches began drifting over the lake. It was downright eerie. Shortly afterward, however, our bodies became completely numb from the cold, and we were able to shut up and get some sleep.

The next morning both Vern and I were a little stiff. He managed to get up before I did, if you can call hobbling around in the fetal position being "up." Then I popped right up, with a little help from Vern. He said he was surprised to find such a good pry pole and fulcrum right there in camp.

"Maybe they were left here just for this purpose," he said.

"Shut up and pry," I said. "I want to be up and about by the time the fish start rising."

Much as I enjoy roughing it in the mountains, I prefer my little pickup camper. It gives me a sense of freedom. It's like having a little house on my back. If I don't want to be where I am, I drive my house off toward where I am not.

The camper also gives me a sense of security I don't get from sleeping out on the hard, cold ground. It's much easier not to believe in Sasquatches, for example, when you're sleeping in a camper. I've noticed that my friend Retch Sweeney will scoff at the notion of Sasquatches while he's in my camper, keep an open mind about them while sleeping in a tent, and put up a good argument for their existence while sleeping out under the stars.

I don't know if Sasquatches exist or not, but I like to think they do. The idea of Sasquatches appeals to me, if not the real thing. I understand that they smell terrible. If Sasquatches didn't exist, how could anyone know what they smell like?

Numerous people report having actually smelled them. Not long ago a couple of backpackers were trekking through the mountains and suddenly a roaring, eight-foot-tall, red-eyed creature with fangs the size of railroad spikes bounded out onto the trail a few feet ahead of them and then vanished into the brush. The backpackers reported that immediately after the sighting they noticed an unpleasant odor. I believe them, too. Indeed, almost all reports of such sightings mention an unpleasant smell. If something smells bad, it must exist, right? I rest my case for the existence of the Sasquatch.

I do a lot of my camping in Sasquatch country. If it

wanted to, I have no doubt that a Sasquatch could rip the
door right off my camper. It could probably roll my camper
and truck right off the side of a mountain. But I am prepared for just such a contingency. Any time I hear a serious
ruckus outside at night, I yell "Red alert! Red alert!" Then
I open the sliding window to the truck cab and my camping
partner swings down out of the top bunk, shoots his legs
through the sliding window and lands in the truck cab in
one easy motion. He then starts up the truck and we drive
off toward someplace we are not, leaving behind the source
of the trouble, whether an irate moose, an angry grizzly, or
a smelly Sasquatch. It's nice.

Sometimes when I plan to camp in one place for several
days, I remove the camper from the truck and set it on a
couple of stout sawhorses. I have a battery pack for the
electrical system, so it's easy to forget, especially coming out
of a deep sleep, that the camper's not on the truck.

One night Retch Sweeney and I were camping up on the
St. Joe and were awakened in the middle of the night by a
racket down the road from us. I got up and looked out the
camper window.

"A gang of bikers just rode in," I said. "They've built
a big fire and are setting up camp."

"Oh, great!" Retch said. "Just what we need—a gang
of bikers camping down the road, and us out in the middle
of nowhere!"

"Maybe they won't notice us," I said. "They probably
wouldn't bother us anyway."

"Fat chance of that!"

"Go back to sleep. They'll probably be gone in the
morning."

No sooner had we dozed off than we heard another disturbance outside the camper. "Red alert!" I shouted to Retch. "Red alert!" I jerked open the sliding window, and Retch in one easy motion swung down and shot himself right out onto the ground. We had forgotten that we'd set the camper on the sawhorses!

"Whazzat?" Retch said. I grabbed a flashlight and shined it out the window so Retch could see better. Well, it was nothing more than a yearling bear cub that had climbed up on a tall black stump next to the camper, trying to reach a chest cooler we had secured to the roof. He was a cute little fellow and didn't seem the least bit afraid.

"Hey, Retch," I called out. "Get a load of this cute little . . ."

"*SASQUATCH!*" Retch screamed. "*SASQUATCH!*"

"Hush!" I said. "It's only a little bear trying to get at our cooler."

But Retch had already streaked off, yelling back at me, "*RUN FOR YOUR LIFE! SASQUATCH! SASQUATCH!*"

Just as I suspected, he had forgotten about the bikers. As he went by their camp, still yelling "*SASQUATCH! SAS-QUATCH!*" they leaped out of their sleeping bags and took off after him. He glanced back and saw that now he was being chased by not only what he imagined to be a Sasquatch but also a murderous gang of bikers he had rudely awakened.

Retch had been doing a lot of running lately and was in terrific shape. He didn't think he would have any trouble outrunning a gang of bikers. So he was pretty surprised when the bikers nearly caught up with him. He leaped off a bank, hurtled some brush, ran through a little creek, and spurted back up on to the road. The bikers stayed tight on his tail all the way. He could see he was going to have a hard time losing these fellows. As he said later, he thought the bikers must have had difficulty finding victims, to put all that effort into catching him. At last Retch tired and slowed to a trot, concluding that a little playful beating-up by the bikers was better than dying of exhaustion. But the bikers shot right on past him. As one hairy chap sprinted by, he shouted at Retch, "Just how big was it, bud?" Before Retch could reply, the biker disappeared into the night.

In the meantime, I loaded the camper back on my truck, and took off after my camping partner.

"What a night!" Retch gasped, once he was safe inside the truck. "First I nearly get nabbed by a Sasquatch and then a gang of bikers chase me two miles through the mountains!"

"Yeah," I said. "Actually, the 'Sasquatch' was only a little bear on a big tree stump. I thought you'd like to know."

Retch stared at me for a moment. "Well, the bikers were real!"

"They were real, all right," I said. "What I can't understand is why they didn't chase you on their bikes. Surely, they could pedal a lot faster than they could run!"

"Pedal?" Retch said. "Pedal!"

We drove on in thoughtful silence through the night, toward someplace we were not.